One of the hardest things to and take a long, hard, and I causing us to do that when v changing, life-threatening situations. Laurie Haughton faced that kind of trauma as she loved and dealt with her son Joshua and his congenital heart defect. With raw honesty she walks us through the ups and down, the joys and fears, the triumphs and the nightmares of both Joshua's fight for life, as well as her own struggles to understand her reactions and the changes in her psyche as she grappled with the "Why, God?" questions we've all had. I highly recommend this book for everyone interested in going on a roller coaster journey of life and faith.

—Barrie Doyle, author of *The Excalibur Parchment* and other novels in the Oak Grove Conspiracies series

This compelling story recounts the journey of author Laurie Haughton and her husband, Tim, as they face the health challenges of their firstborn son, Joshua. It's an exceptionally transparent narrative through which we gain glimpses into their inner struggles to make sense of what was happening and find a way to embrace a deeply uncomfortable reality outside of their control. At the heart of the story is the discovery of the sustaining power of trust in God despite uncertain, unsettling, and unexpected circumstances. The three graces of faith, hope, and love are woven into the fabric of this journey—never denying the difficult realities, but always serving as rays of light in the times of darkness. The book offers eloquent testimony to the vital and nurturing role of human relationships when on a path where risk is high and the potential for loss seems ever present.

Though unique in its details, this account of a very personal journey reaches beyond its particulars and offers valuable insights for any who may be called upon to find their way through darkness and the uncertainties of life.

—John Franklin, Executive Director, IMAGO

Through the Lens of
MOTHERHOOD

Through the Lens of
MOTHERHOOD

Trusting God in Times of Trouble

Laurie Haughton

Foreword by Brian Stiller

THROUGH THE LENS OF MOTHERHOOD
Copyright © 2020 by Laurie Haughton

Scripture quotations taken from the New American Standard Bible®, Copyright © 1960, 1962, 1963, 1968, 1971, 1972, 1973, 1975, 1977, 1995 by The Lockman Foundation. Used by permission.

Printed in Canada

ISBN: 978-1-4866-1916-0
eBook ISBN: 978-1-4866-1917-7

Word Alive Press
119 De Baets Street Winnipeg, MB R2J 3R9
www.wordalivepress.ca

WORD ALIVE
—P R E S S—

MIX
Paper from
responsible sources
FSC
www.fsc.org
FSC® C103567

Cataloguing in Publication information can be obtained from Library and Archives Canada.

DEDICATION

For Tim, the only person I would have wanted to travel through life with. You are the port in the storm, and to say I love you seems too small. Thank you for all of your love and support and for the strong shoulders that carry so much and are still soft enough to lean on.

For Joshua and Kaleb, the two amazing little men who made me a mom. I had no idea I needed you in my life until you were in it, and every day since you joined our family, I've been granted a view into God's love for me. Stay true to your convictions, follow the path God leads you on, and never be afraid to ask me for help. There's nothing that will stop me from loving you. God blessed me with you, and I am so honoured to be given the chance to raise you.

Mom and Dad, you have taught me how to love without conditions. You taught me how to be the parent that I am, the person that I am. Your support and love have made me who I am today, and gotten me through. Thank you for all of it, even when I least deserved it.

.

ACKNOWLEDGEMENTS

JOHN AND HELEN, YOU RAISED A MAN TO BE PROUD OF. HE IS A wonderful leader of the church, a strong and faithful husband, and a source of deep strength. Thank you for all of the help you have given us as we travelled this road. Thank you for packing up your lives to come and be of service in our time of need. We love you and appreciate all the things you do.

Alex Newman, I gave you the first glance into my heart, and I was terrified. You read my words, and you not only didn't judge me, but you spoke words of love and support. Thank you for being willing to take the time to edit this book and point out with insight the things I missed along the way. I appreciate you.

FOREWORD

C. S. Lewis in *The Problem of Pain* draws a map pointing us toward an understanding of pain, its origins, and effects. He identifies the problem this way:

> If God were good, He would wish to make His creatures perfectly happy, and if God were almighty He would be able to do what He wished. But the creatures are not happy. Therefore God lacks either goodness, or power, or both. This is the problem of pain in its simplest forms.[1]

Inevitably, all of us on our human journey experience pain. And we all look for a reason that we may never find.

I have cried with those whose joyful expectations have been dashed by a stillbirth, and also with parents whose child, seemingly healthy at birth, develops a deformity or is diminished in mental or physical ability. I suspect that you too have shed tears of sorrow and pain as

---

[1] C.S. Lewis, *The Problem of Pain,* (New York, NY: Macmillan, 1945), 14.

life has delivered something different than what you had hoped for or planned on.

Here in this extraordinary book of personal pain, and with both detailed and descriptive language, Laurie lets us in on her inner and honest feelings. Reading her account of health issues with their two sons, Joshua and Kaleb, is like riding a roller coaster. There are happy surprises, but mostly we join her as she invites us to see and feel her very human struggle.

There are three reasons why this book may be helpful to those experiencing personal pain. First, we learn the details of their medical journey. These provide a context to the emotional drama. This was important for me to become acquainted with what Laurie and her husband were facing, especially with Joshua. Even if it seems overly detailed, I encourage you to stay with the story, for it frames the tough and honest questions Laurie is asking about herself and her faith.

The second reason is that Laurie gives us time to think about our own concerns and questions, to reflect on how we personally view pain. It's instinctive to seek a reason, a cause, or even to blame it all on God. Laurie pondered such questions.

Finally, this book has enormous value in that Laurie provides no easy answers, and neither does she allow us to coast without thinking about how we handle our issues of suffering. Our instinct is to assume that because God is good and we love Him, misadventures and troubling experiences will not be part of our journey. Or for some, that God's promises and presence preclude us from pain and suffering.

But because we live in a real and troubled world, God's love for us does not mean we're exempt from inevitable pain and, in this case, physical defects that randomly affect our lives. It's within this broken creation that God speaks his words of life and love. Again, it is Lewis (*The Problem of Pain*) who reminds us that "God whispers to us in our pleasures, speaks in our conscience, but shouts in our pain: it is His megaphone to rouse a deaf world."

As a mother, Laurie feels deeply the struggles of her sons. Joshua becomes a young life through which we gain insight into how Laurie deals with her aspirations and doubts. As she opens her personal life, we as fellow wanderers are allowed to also navigate our own personal pain and loss. As you read, you will be challenged by her honesty, humility, and understanding.

—Brian C. Stiller
Global Ambassador, the World Evangelical Alliance

PROLOGUE

I'VE ALWAYS LOVED ART AND LONGED TO BE ABLE TO RECREATE IT FOR ALL to see, but I wasn't blessed with great talent in the painting department. Whatever I put to paper was disappointing, or worse, a warped and ugly misrepresentation. But then one day someone placed a camera in my hands, and that all changed. I was at last able to create beauty just as my eyes saw it and, more importantly, share it with the world. I would see things that some might consider old or ugly, but with a slight shift of perception or camera angle, I could render them new and beautiful. It was in the turning of the lens that I was able to find and show the essence of beauty in all of creation.

Nowhere was that truer than in my journey of motherhood. It was like a wide-angle lens that expanded and allowed me a new view of life and God. Things were crisper, clearer, and much more beautiful than I'd realized.

This is the story of our foray into parenthood, but it's also my story of shifting the angles and perceptions and discovering God through the lens of motherhood. I've been writing a blog for many years, but as I read through previous entries, I realized that it's a finite vehicle without the emotional or spiritual room necessary to share all that life has shown me and all that God has revealed to me about himself, his love, and his desire to meet me at the cross.

This book is an attempt to share my story by drawing on the blog posts but also adding some reflections as I look back on those early days with a very ill child. I'm not a scholar or a theologian; I am a mother and a wife. I don't pretend to have the answers to life's questions; I only want to share what I've learned in my walk thus far. I invite you to join me on the walk that took me from the halls of Mt. Sinai Hospital to the waiting room of the cardiac critical care unit at The Hospital for Sick children (SickKids) in Toronto, where I faced some painful questions: Will my son live? Will he take a breath at birth, or suffer for a time before we lose him? If he lives, what will his life look like? How will I face the answers to these questions with my faith, marriage, and life intact?

Having a critically ill child steals the joy and laughter from a time in life when you should be enjoying the new discoveries of parenthood. The air seems thinner, and it's difficult to take full, deep breaths. You can't sleep for more than an hour at a time, because you don't want to miss a thing. You fear that you won't be there for something really good, or something that will change your life forever. You can't concentrate, you find it hard to talk, you ache in the deepest parts of your soul, and fear is your constant companion.

In my journey, I discovered not only the joy and fear that is motherhood, but the hope that comes from God alone. I walked the difficult path that can lead to a life full of love, laughter, and joy but also pain, suffering, and brokenness. I've been blessed with the love of a good man who encourages me, dreams with me, fears with me, and still laughs with me. I'd like to take you on the road with us as we began parenthood, what it meant to us, what we learned about God's gifts and constancy, what we were taught about the cross, and the hope that we found there.

We received a crash course in trust. But the more I hear stories from others, and the more I dig into the Bible, the more I realize that we were never promised a life free from pain or hardship, or one of bliss and success. We have been promised peace during times of trouble, hope and comfort during our darkest hours, and an eternity of love when the end of life comes.

If our story can offer hope, encouragement, and faith to just one person, then I have to say "thank you" to God for that. If you read this and find yourself looking to the cross for your hope, then in my heart I can know that there was purpose in my hardships. I can rejoice in the pain and be encouraged and lifted up in the deepest part of my heart. I can know that I would do it again, because it would be worth it.

ONE

"What are you afraid of?"

LOADED QUESTION, I THINK AS I STARE AT THE BLANK, BEIGE WALL AND search in vain for the answer to somehow reveal itself to me. If I really knew the answer to that, I wouldn't be here—a forty-plus woman who woke up one day unable to recognize herself, a woman lost, a woman so hidden she's almost completely gone. The wall stares back at me; the dull, brownish-white colour reminds me of watered-down, overly-milky gas station coffee that was left too long in the pot. The thought of coffee reminds me of the cup I'm holding, and slowly I lift it to my lips and sip. I turn and look into the gentle eyes of my therapist and shrug at him. "If I knew that, I wouldn't be here. I wouldn't need you to fix me."

He smiles, a kind if not patronizing smile, and his pen moves across the notebook in his lap. I feel like making a joke, saying something to make him like me, but there's nothing. I've got nothing. I look down at my hands, the half-empty coffee is swaying in the paper cup, and I realize that I'm shaking. This is not where I was supposed to end up, sitting in a dingy office with a guy paid to listen to me. I had been on a different path. I was the strong one, the brave one. Or was I?

The coffee is lukewarm, but I keep sipping so that I have something to do, something to fill the awkwardness of sitting in front of this stranger and being expected to bare it all. He's watching me. I can feel his eyes on me, feel him waiting. I put the coffee down and look at him. Our eyes meet and I smile. "You'll have to ask me more directed questions. Let's get this started." He smiles a real smile this time and puts the pen down in his lap as we begin.

The first time I ever met Tim—on July 21, 2006—I had a feeling that this was the one I'd waited so long for. There was no way to explain it, and believe me, I tried to when my single friends asked. We'd met online through a Christian dating website. Had you told me years ago that this was how I'd meet my husband, I wouldn't have believed it. I'd just moved home from Austria after several years away, and all my previous friends had scattered elsewhere. I attended a church full of my parents' friends who were much older than me. Tim was a pastor, spent most of his time at church and with his parishioners, and couldn't date people in his church. So how do you meet people?

I wasn't interested in dating too seriously, since I was recovering from a broken engagement in Europe. Although dating sounded like fun, it wasn't something I was ready to embrace, so I only took out a free seven-day membership on the site. I met some very strange people who, even though they called themselves believers, didn't seem to live out or believe the same things I did. So at the end of my seven days, I bowed out and didn't return. Tim, on the other hand, paid for his membership and had some very similar types of dates.

Driving to visit my parents in May of 2006, I heard an almost audible voice telling me that God had a pastor in mind for me. My stomach turned—I was not a good candidate to be a pastor's wife. In fact, much later, when one man who knew me well learned I was to marry a pastor, he laughed and said, "God certainly has a sense of humour." Recently, I was told that being a pastor's wife is a calling. I thought back to this experience and realized they were right. God was definitely calling me that day.

My heart had always been rebellious and angry, and my teen years were a nightmare for my parents. The thought of being a pastor's wife actually brought fear to my heart. It didn't make any sense to me, but in a moment of clarity, I realized that throughout my life I'd felt my safest and most secure and content when I was on the path God had for me. If God wanted me to be a pastor's wife, then he sure had a lot of work to do in me, but I was willing to let him chisel away and see what the sculpture turned into.

I decided that since God already had someone picked out for me, I could take a break from looking and just enjoy the upcoming summer. I spent a lot of time at the cottage with my parents, whom I'd missed while living in Europe. I also reconnected with myself and with God. It was a lonely time but fruitful as well. One weekend as I sat on the beach at the cottage, I felt God speaking to me about dating a divorced man. That had always been something I would never consider. I didn't want the headache of an ex and possibly children. To be honest, I wanted to be someone's first wife, not someone's second choice.

On Monday night I returned to the city. I'd only been home a short time before I got a phone call from a friend I'd known in Austria who now lived just few hours' drive away. She was going on a date with someone from the same website I'd been on, and she wanted me to look at his profile and give her my opinion. I told her that I wasn't on the site anymore, so we continued to talk about other things while I checked my email from the weekend. I was quite surprised when I opened my inbox to find an email from the same website saying "We miss you" and giving me another three free days. I signed in to see the profile of my friend's date. After discussing the guy, his picture, and his profile, we began to peruse the other profiles.

That's when I saw this handsome face smiling at me. I was so taken with his smile, and with the second picture in which he was holding a small African child, that I wrote to him immediately. I didn't think anything else of it for a few minutes while my friend and I chatted, but then I got an instant message from this very same person who was smiling at me earlier. We chatted for quite a while, and I explained that I was not a member, nor would I be, of that website. He gave me his contact information, and we took up chatting on MSN Messenger.

We talked long into the night about so many things. When I woke up in the morning and started up my computer, I found another little note from him. And so it went for the rest of the day. We worked and chatted all day and again the following day. On the third day I got a shock. He was a pastor and divorced. My heart sank. Divorced was exactly what I didn't want, but when I asked what had happened, I learned that his reasons for divorcing were biblical. We talked theology, as I wanted to know if he was on the same wavelength as me spiritually. He was. We didn't want to waste time writing to each other for months on end if we weren't going to connect in person at the end of it all, so we decided to meet that Friday at a coffee shop down the street from my apartment.

When I drove into the parking lot that night, Tim was already there, leaning against his motorcycle and waiting for me. I remember thinking how attractive he was, how nice, how well he seemed to listen, and how many echoes we shared in our spiritual lives. God was speaking to us, using the same language, using the same story—the wonderful story of Abraham, Sarah, Isaac, and Ishmael. I trusted him in a way that I'd never trusted a man, especially one I had just met. We literally talked for hours that night, and we saw each other regularly from that time on.

One night I lay in bed, afraid of my feelings for Tim and of the pain that would come if those feelings weren't returned. I'd been in serious relationships before, including a broken engagement, and the last thing I needed was another "not too serious" relationship. I was in a contented place where I would rather not date than end up in another dead-end relationship.

Tim and I had agreed to give the relationship six months and see where it was leading, so that we wouldn't waste each other's time if it wasn't going to work. That night as I lay in bed, afraid of the future, I said a quiet prayer, asking that God either confirm my growing feelings or give my spirit unrest if the relationship wasn't right. I fell asleep confident that something would work out.

The next night, Tim told me that he loved me, and I felt the presence of God so clearly that there was no doubt he was sitting between us. I went to bed that night knowing that this was the man

I would spend my life with. This was the man God had been saving for me and preparing me for. I had finally met him, and my blood bubbled with excitement!

On December 8, 2006, we went to cut down a Christmas tree and decorate it in preparation for a party he was hosting for the youth group on Sunday afternoon. We baked cookies and trimmed the tree. After we finished, Tim made a fondue supper and laid a fire, and we had a romantic evening together. Tim pulled out his guitar and started to sing a song he'd written for me, one that ended in a request to marry him. I almost forgot to answer him, I was so happy.

We got married four months later on April 28, 2007. It was a short dating relationship, but I have never doubted that this was ordained by God and that we were completely within his will. This was my best friend, my lover, and the man who would partner with me in the journey of life. Someone once asked me, "If you knew then what you know now, would you have still said yes?" My answer was and will remain, "I would have done it sooner!" I have no hesitations or doubts, only love and respect for the man God chose for me. The only question left unanswered was how I'd found favour in God's eyes for such a miracle.

TWO

"Having a child fills a hole in your heart
that you didn't even know was empty."
~Anonymous~

FROM THE MOMENT YOU KNOW ABOUT THE LITTLE CHILD GROWING
inside of you, you think about them and dream about what they will look
like, what their talents will be, what they will sound like, and what it will
feel like to hold them for the first time and hear them say "mommy" or
"daddy" for the first time. We carry these hopes and dreams even before
the moment of conception or the knowledge that we're expecting. The
idea of being a parent is foreign until it's upon you, and then, before you
know it, you love those little beings before they're even here. You want to
protect them, give them the best, and make a way for them in the world
that's as easy as possible.

On July 1, 2007, Tim and I found out that we were going to be
parents for the first time. We both cried when we saw the results staring
up at us from the little stick. For days we were in a blissful place of
dreams and joy. I barely slept, thinking about what this sweet little baby
would look like, what he would enjoy, and what kinds of things would
make him laugh. As the pregnancy wore on and my tummy grew, the
excitement mingled with fear and discomfort, but still there was much

joy. The first time I felt my baby move inside me was such an amazing feeling, I began to crave it. Those first few months were so precious to us … to me. I will never forget the first time Tim felt the baby move. I was lying on the couch and he started to kick, so Tim came over and put his head on my tummy. The baby gave a powerful kick and Tim, startled, looked up at me and said, "Are you freaking kidding me?" The look of awe and wonder on his face was beautiful!

It didn't take long for the joy and anticipation to turn to fear, concern, and worry. At my twenty-week ultrasound, the doctor noticed a two-vessel cord rather than the normal three-vessel cord, so they wanted to get a better look. At the same ultrasound, we discovered that we were having a boy. With tears streaming down our cheeks, we named him Joshua.

I was sent for a stage two ultrasound but was told that it was probably nothing and not to be too concerned. However, the anomaly showed up as a ballooning valve, so a fetal echocardiogram (echo) was ordered at SickKids in Toronto. I was terrified. What did it all mean? What's a ballooning valve? That can't be too serious, right? We began to pray, and God impressed upon me Joshua 1:9: *"Have I not commanded you? Be strong and courageous! Do not tremble or be afraid, for the Lord God is with you wherever you go."*

I don't know about you, but that kind of verse isn't all that comforting. I mean, when God says "Don't be afraid; I am with you," it usually means there's something to be nervous about. I began to pray that God would help me understand, comfort me, and give me the courage I lacked. Then I read Matthew 19:26: *"And looking at them Jesus said to them, 'With people this is impossible, but with God all things are possible."* Now that brought comfort! It felt like I'd been given a promise directly from God himself, and I believed. God would save our Joshua; he would perform a miracle for us. Joshua's name means "God saves," and I believed with all my heart that it was God who had named our son, and that He would save him.

The morning of our fetal echo dawned, and we went to the hospital feeling hopeful and light in spirit. This was going to be nothing! We chatted with each other throughout the procedure and watched Joshua's heart beating with rapt attention. I'm not a doctor, nor am I an X-ray technician, but his heart was beating. That was good, right? After an hour of pushing and prodding at my tummy, the technician stood up and said that he would show the pictures to the doctor and we'd be finished unless they needed more pictures. Tim and I sat in the room— Tim spinning around on the technician's swivel chair in boredom, and me quietly feeling the bumps, kicks, and hiccups of my son. Tim wandered around the area and came back after a few moments to tell me about a small room across the hall.

"It's so sad," he said. "There's a table, a couple of chairs, a model heart, and a box of tissues."

The doctor and technician came back; they needed more pictures, so I resumed the position on the table, and they squirted cold jelly onto my belly once more. Tim took up his spot at the foot of the bed, and we shared a look of trepidation. They finished the last few pictures and told me I could get dressed. They asked us to wait in the waiting room, or at least that's what I heard. We went to the waiting room, and the doctor said, "No, in here, please." He then directed us to the same room Tim had seen earlier. We were now the people sitting in this "counselling room." The model heart was the most prominent feature of the room— that and the box of tissues. It was one of the smallest rooms I've ever been in. The walls were close; the air, thin. Taking a deep breath was difficult, almost like being on a mountain peak with little oxygen.

The doctor came back in. He smiled and introduced himself, shaking our hands. He must have seen that my hands were shaking and my skin had become clammy. I found myself feeling slightly embarrassed about it. Tim made a joke, something about the room, but the doctor didn't smile. That made the knot in my stomach grow tighter. Then he started to talk, and I was lost in the scientific words that made up the heart of my firstborn. Something about valves, large muscle mass, possible death, blah, blah blah, SickKids Hospital.

The scientific terminology went like this: Pulmonary atresia with intact ventricular septum (PAIVS) is a rare congenital cardiac lesion characterized by heterogeneous right ventricular development, an imperforate pulmonary valve, and possible extensive ventriculocoronary connections. Prognosis and management depend on the degree of right ventricular hyperplasia (including tricuspid valve hyperplasia) and the dependency of the myocardial blood supply on abnormal communications between the right ventricle and coronary arteries.

I was lost in a sea of practical matters that didn't matter at all.

"Will I be able to keep my midwife?"

No, I was being reassigned to the special pregnancy unit at Mt. Sinai Hospital.

"Will I be able to take him home right away?"

Not likely; he will need to be transferred to SickKids following his birth.

"Will I be able to breastfeed right away?"

Possibly.

What I really wanted to know but was too afraid to ask was, "Will my life ever be the same after this conversation?" In my heart I knew the answer. Life would never again be the same; this pregnancy would never be the same. The time for joy and rejoicing had been stolen from us. Tim asked all the right questions, the ones that really mattered. He seemed to understand what was happening, and he seemed to be calm in the raging wind that was threatening to knock me off balance.

There were a few years of my life when I lived in Austria, in a small mountain town not far from Zell-am-See in the heart of the Alps. There wasn't much there, and to get to any big city was a major endeavour. We took up hitchhiking to get around. At that time, we needed to leave the country every three months to get our visas renewed. There came a time when a friend of mine and I decided to take a little bit of a holiday to do this, instead of the typical quick drive across the border and back. After some research, we decided to hitchhike to Budapest, Hungary (about a fourteen-hour drive). I think back on the decision and thank God that I survived it, wondering at the stupidity that allowed us to make that choice. But there's a part of me that still thrills at the experience. We had a number of exciting experiences; we met some really fun people, some rather strange people, and even some creepy people.

What brings me back to this trip right now is one particular ride. We were heading home after a week in Budapest; our time was running out, and we needed to get back to work. This didn't allow time for a lot of discretion when accepting rides. We were also on the highway, which is a big no-no in the hitchhiking world, and also illegal. You can hitch a ride at exits and on ramps but never on the highway itself. So here we were, dumped on the highway by one of the few "odd" people we'd met, and desperate for a ride. We stood there, thumbs outstretched, and a prayer in our heart that a car would stop before the police came.

We didn't wait long before a van stopped a number of feet ahead of us. We grabbed our gear and ran up it. We peered through the window and then glanced at each other. Inside the van were nine Greek men, none of whom spoke English and only a little German. I remember questioning our sanity right before we got into the van and they shut the door. I sat in the very back row, and my friend sat in front of me; both of us were sandwiched between the men. The driver, for some reason, didn't feel it necessary to watch the road and chose instead to turn around and speak to us in his very limited German. My heart was racing. The man beside me started to rub my hair; I sat on the edge of my seat as I felt the panic rise into my throat.

That feeling, or panic, of facing some unknown threat was how I felt that day in the hospital listening to this man's dire talk about valves and ventricles and prognoses. My heart sped up, my throat tightened, and fear made my limbs tingle. How did it come to this? This was supposed to happen to other people, those people on the telethon for SickKids. This doesn't happen to people like Tim and me, and it certainly doesn't happen to our children. Does it?

It wasn't until much later that I really understood what had been said in that meeting, and only then because Tim explained it to me so many times, and I had a diagram from the doctor. If only head knowledge translated so easily to the heart. Joshua had been diagnosed with pulmonary atresia, a condition in which the pulmonary valve hasn't formed and is completely blocked, making it impossible after birth for the blood to pump properly. Upon birth he would need to have a balloon dilation (where they basically shove a catheter all the way up to his heart from his groin area and blow a hole through the valve so that blood can move freely). It seems so simple, yet a part of me didn't fully grasp the complexity of the issue. The doctor had said that it could be as simple as one procedure and then nothing ever again, or it could ultimately cause death. There was no way of knowing what to expect until he was born, but we knew with certainty that there would be no miracles here. This was not going to go away. Those were the doctor's words, not mine, but I clung to them, figuring that when people throw challenges like that out to God, he will surely perform the miracle just to show them that miracles *do* happen. Right? I clung to that hope as my security, because God had told me that nothing was impossible with him.

Something in my heart changed that day regarding the pregnancy; I think Tim changed too. The joy and excitement were gone, the wonder and anticipation of seeing our child for the first time became a thing to be feared, and a cloud hanging over our home threatened our peace and our future. Our lives became endless rounds of medical appointments, ultrasounds, meetings with social workers, hospital tours, and talks with expressionless doctors telling us to prepare for the death of our son. Even worse were the doctors who repeatedly advised an abortion so that we wouldn't suffer. That sickened us. We were prepared to fight for the life of our son, and those in charge of his care were telling us not to bother, to just get rid of him. We kept explaining that this was our son they were talking about killing, but they didn't seem to understand.

Tim eventually leaned forward and said to the doctor: "Is there somewhere you can write in that file that I never want to have this conversation again?" The doctor was flustered. He explained that it was his legal responsibility to bring it up, which felt to us like they were more concerned about the legal situation than about the life they were trained and being paid to save. One doctor, after being informed that we would not abort, told us to bring a camera to labour and delivery, because it could be our only chance of getting a photo of him. He then advised us to discuss whether to have an autopsy or not on the drive home that day.

That dark period had a few bright moments. During the ultrasounds, we could watch him on the screen, growing and moving. He moved a lot! We could make out little feet, little hands, his nose; he was so sweet, even in 2D black and white.

The day of our second fetal echo loomed before us. I prayed harder than I ever had before, and always the same thing came into my mind: "Do not be afraid. I am with you wherever you go; nothing is impossible with God." I knew that somehow, some way, God would allow my son to live. Somehow Joshua would survive, despite the dire predictions of his many doctors. I began to dream and imagine that on the day of the second fetal echo, the doctor who had said there would be no miracles would look down at those pictures in awe and see a perfectly formed pulmonary valve. I began to believe that was the miracle we would receive. I believed so much in that miracle that I actually began to look forward to that moment and pictured all the ways I would tell that doctor about the God who had performed the miracle.

The morning of the echo came, and after a sleepless night, we finally gave up at six in the morning and began to prepare for the appointment. We went into the nursery that we had prepared for Joshua, and I sat in the rocking chair. Tim walked around me seven times, just as Joshua had walked around Jericho. On the seventh time, he blew a horn, just as Joshua had done, and then we prayed. We prayed that just as God had torn the walls of Jericho down, he would tear through the wall of the pulmonary valve. Then, after our prayer, fully believing that a miracle had happened, we got in the car and headed to the SickKids echo lab.

Fetal echoes are ultrasounds that zoom in a million times more than a regular picture. You can see every little thing happening in the baby's heart. The technician sat hunched over, mumbling to himself about measurements and whatnot. Tim took up his position at the end of the bed, squeezing my feet three times to say "I love you" and reassure me. I just lay there, trying hard to remember not to gloat at the doctor. Gloating isn't a good way to share the love of the Lord of miracles. I had to remember that this man had said "no miracles here" out of ignorance, not malice. I had to be kind, patient, and loving when he revealed his mistake. Over and over it went through my head, imagining that moment in anticipation.

This time we were ready to be asked to sit in the counselling room, so it wasn't quite as daunting as the previous time. This time I noticed, for example, that the room wasn't as small as I'd imagined. It had a filing cabinet at one end and a bookshelf at the other. The table was round and there was room for four chairs and a stroller. The door had a window in it, and the air didn't seem as thin. The lights even seemed brighter, although I guess they could have changed the wattage since we'd been there last. Tim and I chatted while we waited for the doctor to come back in with our file. We talked about mundane things, like where we'd have lunch and what we'd do with the rest of the day. Only occasionally did I have a flutter of nerves in my tummy, just the smallest of shadows crossing overhead.

The doctor returned, but instead of the triumphant sounds of victory, I heard the troubadour of sorrow. There had been no miracle that morning. His heart was not better; there had been no tearing down of the walls of Jericho. I didn't hear another word of that appointment. My heart ached, and the cloud that I had been only vaguely aware of earlier became a large storm, gathering and threatening to shake me to the core.

THREE

"Faith can move mountains,
and your doubt can create them"
~ Anonymous~

I ONCE BELIEVED THAT FAITH THE SIZE OF A MUSTARD SEED WOULD MOVE
a mountain; in fact, my signature on every email was "Walking on a
path of mustard seeds," because I literally walk on faith to get through
life. That day, in that small office, I slipped off the path of mustard seeds!
I had believed, even when no one else thought it was possible—I had
still believed. I'm sure people thought I was in denial, or that I was being
hormonal, possibly even delusional, but it wasn't that. I fully, without
doubt or question, had believed that God would fix that valve, that he
would make the muscle mass less thick, and that the doctor would have
to eat his words. Where had I gone wrong? At what point had I let doubt
in and caused my faith to not be enough?

When you go through a challenging time in life, you will always get
the well-meaning people who come up to you, pat you on the shoulder,
and say, "You just need to have faith; he'll make it all better." I heard it
so much after this point that every time someone said it, I had to resist
screaming. I had faith, but either I didn't have enough, or God just
didn't care about me, because it didn't work. Joshua was still sick. Anger

and doubt began to inch into my life, fear began to claw its way into my heart, and I began to lie awake at night, afraid to sleep because when sleep came, it always brought nightmares.

I am the pastor's wife; people look to him and me as examples. We aren't supposed to falter. We aren't supposed to fall. We live public lives in so many ways, and this was one of them. People feel a sense of ownership over him, and by association, over me. Everyone knows us because of his job, and because of his job, many expect high standards of faith and morality. I knew what I was getting into before marriage. I was fully aware of what would and wouldn't be expected of me, and I happily signed the marriage certificate. The reality, though, of trying to suffer the doubts and frailties of life in plain view of those who are either looking to you for guidance or waiting for you to fail is something no one can prepare you for. There's an added element to suffering because you keep it quiet, hide your doubts, stifle your anger, and weather the storms with a smile on your face, hoping nobody notices the perilous fault line you're walking on.

I don't know how it happened, but I slowly closed up. No longer open and warm, I began to hide; I began to pretend. I didn't want pity, and I became angry when people said they were so sorry about my son, because I wasn't sorry. He was my son. I wanted him and I loved him, so why would I be sorry about him? No one understood except Tim, but even he didn't have the same feelings for Joshua at that time that I did. I felt alone, more alone than I'd ever felt in my life. People would ask how I was doing, and I'd smile and say that I was fine, that everything was okay. What was the point of telling them how I felt? Would they understand? Did they really want the truth? I could barely put it into words myself, let alone tell someone else how I was feeling, how I was coping, or what was going on in my head. Was I okay? I don't think I even knew that I wasn't. What's worse, I didn't realize then how "not okay" I really was.

Something happens when you become a mother. Suddenly, your world shifts, and you're no longer at the centre of it—this new life is. Everything you want, everything you feel, everything you do becomes secondary to your child. You make them your centre, and regardless of whether that's right or even healthy, it happens. This little life is put into your care, and you get a God-complex, believing that you are solely responsible for their well-being, their happiness, and ultimately for how they turn out.

This is usually the point when God slaps you up-side the head and reminds you that he alone is God and he needs to be the centre. God didn't smack me in the head until much later, though; he allowed me to move along in this lie for quite some time. Like a serious illness, it took over completely. I started to believe that it must somehow be my fault. Had I eaten something bad at the beginning of the pregnancy? Had I done something in the past that had caused this? Had I committed some wrong that I was being punished for? I began to bargain with God, begging him to make Joshua well at all costs. I used all the manipulation tools I had in my arsenal. And when you're fighting or bargaining for your baby's life, those tools are considerable.

On January 1, 2008, the first day of a new year, a day when most people are starting fresh and looking forward with hope to a year of exciting things, Tim and I were at the hospital with a friend in pretty serious condition. As you can imagine, after New Year's Eve the waiting room was standing room only, and the mood was dark. I grew very tired, and things didn't feel right. Desperate to lie down but with nowhere to do so, I went to the parking lot and got into the car. Within minutes, I was asleep. I felt so strange. Something was definitely wrong, but I couldn't do anything about it. Yes, we were at the hospital, but the situation that had brought us there concerned someone else, not me, nor could I make it about me. I knew that I had to wait it out, see if I felt better or worse in time. Hours later, when we were able to go home, we walked in the door and I lay down on the couch. Poor Tim was so tired, how could I tell him that I needed to return to the hospital? I waited a bit before saying anything, but soon we were back in the car and headed for Mt. Sinai Hospital.

I don't know what we were expecting that day, but I wasn't expecting what happened. They took me in right away, did a bedside ultrasound, and called the doctor. Joshua wasn't moving; his heart rate was all over the place, dipping to crazy lows and reaching insane heights. Everything happened quickly after that, with doctors coming and going, telling Tim that they would need to take the baby that night. We were terrified that Joshua was still too small to survive at just thirty weeks with a heart condition. It was surreal, almost like I was out of my body watching it all happen around me. We asked to speak with a pediatrician for advice, but when he came in, he brought fairly dire news. There was no way that at this stage of gestation, with his heart issues, Joshua could survive the birth. If they took him out that night, we were going to lose our son.

At that point I stopped listening and began to pray in a way that I haven't before and only have a few times since. It was simple. Let this baby live. No other words, no bargaining, no manipulating, just those four words: let this baby live. Peace came; I felt it for the first time since that day the cloud took over in the counselling room. God was there; regardless of the outcome, God wouldn't leave me alone. I had to be brave. I wasn't alone, and he could do the impossible.

The doctor who had wanted to perform the C-section left to consult with the pediatrician, and they felt that they had to try to keep the baby inside longer. They gave me medication to stop labour and injected me in the hip with a steroid that would help Joshua's lungs develop should they need to take him early. Then, as quickly as they had come, they left, and Tim and I were alone. We could hear the monitors and beeps and the quiet hum of the hospital in the background. We just looked at each other with wide eyes. What insane world had we just entered? What was happening to us? What was happening to Joshua? Why? It was like a crazy episode of the medical drama *Grey's Anatomy*. I was just waiting for the star doctor, McDreamy to walk in and for someone to yell "Cut!"

The next day I was given a non-stress test, which is the *biggest* oxymoron I've ever heard. You lie on a table, and a monitor is strapped around your middle, making it impossible to move. Then they leave you alone and you have nothing to do but watch the monitor and your baby's heart rate and movements, all being spit out on a long piece of paper that you don't understand and can't read. Not exactly a recipe for "non-stressing."

The days folded into one another, one the same as the next. I was hormonal and scared and tired and bored. I slept badly and had to wait until Tim could get to the hospital to have any caffeine. Tim bought me a DVD player, and that became my new best friend. Every morning I had to go for a "non"-stress test, and every afternoon I had an ultrasound. It was both monotonous and scary, and all I wanted was to go home. On the third or fourth afternoon during yet another ultrasound, the technician started to get really rough. She was poking me and prodding at my tummy, and she looked concerned. She said it looked like I might be having the baby that day. Seeing the look of fear on my face, she then smiled and said, "It's okay. He'll be big enough to survive; you just don't have a friendly womb."

I was hurt and angry with the nurse, but the truth was that I was angry with myself. My body was betraying my baby, and I was failing at the most important job of my life, a job I hadn't even really gotten started on—motherhood. I was shuttled back to my room to await a doctor. When I got there, Tim was waiting. We again began to pray. We didn't know what was going on, just that I had an unfriendly womb, whatever that meant.

We were moved back to a labour and delivery room instead of the nice and reasonably comfortable bed in the maternity ward. A doctor came in carrying a portable ultrasound machine and explained that the baby wasn't moving. They began the ultrasound, and you could hear a pin drop, the tension in the room was so palpable. I was scared to breathe. The screen showed Joshua's whole body, and he wasn't moving. Not even a little bit. If not for his heartbeat, we would have thought he was gone. We watched intently, not even looking away long enough to blink, willing him to roll over, kick, fight, to do something, anything. The doctor pushed my tummy hard, and we could see the probe on the screen pushing into Joshua, but still he didn't move. We could see that the doctor was worried. I was scared to look at Tim, but I clung to his hand. Joshua's heart rate was up and down. It wasn't looking very good, and for a moment I really thought, *This is the only living photo I will see of my son.*

Just as the doctor was probing deeply for the last time and explaining that he would need to take him out via C-section and try to give him a chance outside the womb, Joshua began to fight (cue victorious music).

We watched the screen as his little arm shot out and punched right where the doctor's probe was pushing into him. It was just like a scene out of *Rocky*! Tim took a deep breath beside me. I felt it hot against my neck, and with a triumphant pride, he said, "That's my boy!" I couldn't speak past the tears of relief. I took a deep breath myself and lay back on the bed. We would have more time. Joshua wasn't ready to meet us yet. My job, or shall we say my mission, became keeping Joshua inside of me until the thirty-six-week mark, when he would viable.

FOUR

ANGER AND I WERE BECOMING FRIENDS THROUGHOUT THIS PREGNANCY, although I didn't really know it at the time—or maybe I did, but I ignored it, afraid of its potential impact. I've only now started learning how deep and ingrained the anger is, starting as a seed back when God didn't pull out the miracle I'd been longing for and, frankly, expecting. My theology had become warped, and my prayer life was flat and spiritless. If he wasn't listening, why bother talking? This was so subtle at first, because I was still praying and waiting for that miracle while lying to myself by saying that I wasn't angry about it going unfulfilled. I lied to others when I said I was fine and that I still believed God would come through and save Joshua, returning everything to normal. Against everyone's advice, I prepared his nursery. I put his name up on the wall and placed sheets on the bed, with a bear sitting in the corner just waiting for arms to hold him. I grew angry with the many doctors who still told us to abort, to try again at another time, to give up.

In Canada, it's legal to abort your child right into the ninth month of pregnancy. As long as that baby doesn't take one breath outside the womb, you're able to kill it. As soon as that same baby takes a breath outside the womb, then killing it is murder. I am not a scholar, but this just doesn't make any sense to me. On occasion, I try to understand the logic behind it, but I can't. On one day I can abort him and toss him in a garbage bag marked "medical waste," but on the next, after he's born, I'll be considered the worst kind of murderer, a baby killer, if I do the same thing.

But this isn't a book about abortion, so I'll stop here and simply say that I got angry with the doctors, the technicians, the people who loved me, and with myself for not being the kind of mother who could breed a healthy child in my "unfriendly" womb. The only person I couldn't admit to being angry with was God. Doing that might incur his wrath, and Joshua needed God on my side, so I couldn't do that. As I write this out, I see how warped and crazy it is to think, let alone write down, for the world to see. So quietly was it whispered into my ear that I didn't know until the seed had taken root and sprouted.

I went into nesting mode once I got home from the hospital— cleaning, organizing, folding cute little clothes. I tried to pick the perfect outfit to bring him home in, but they were all so sweet, I couldn't choose. I relaxed, rested, and played housewife. I had bi-weekly appointments with my doctor and regular ultrasounds. Life was fairly routine for a few weeks, with tests and more tests marking my calendar, followed up by rest and time with Tim, preparing to be parents.

Our OB was good, never pushing the idea of abortion on us, especially after we made it clear for the fourth time that we would not be choosing that route. He was also very laid-back and relaxed, which gave me a sense of calm. If he wasn't freaking out, then everything would be okay. In fact, sometimes he was so relaxed, we wondered if maybe he shouldn't be freaking out just a little bit. Everyone at SickKids was telling us to book an induction so that we'd be assured of a bed. They told us horror stories of families whose child had to be flown to Boston Children's because SickKids hadn't had a bed available, but Dr. R. was in no hurry. "There will be beds," he would say. "No worries." We were worried about everything by then but also oddly calmed by his lack of real concern.

On Wednesday, January 30, 2008, Dr. R. finally decided that it would be good to book the induction. We scheduled it for three weeks later. I have to admit, I didn't feel ready to be a mom, nor did I feel ready to handle all that we would need to cope with. But at the same time, there was a light at the end of the tunnel, hope in the idea that there was a date, a time picked by the doctor, for Joshua to arrive. Surely the doctor wouldn't take him before his time.

Everything was going to be okay after all. There was an ending in sight, a resolution of sorts, because we'd finally know how this dramatic movie we'd found ourselves in would turn out. I would no longer have to lie in bed at night wondering if the little boy growing inside of me would live to see our faces, know our touch, or hear my words of love. In just three weeks, I would know. And if that was scary, it had to be less scary than the unknown.

I once burned my leg very badly with a heating pad. My knees had been so sore, and I was unable to sleep, so I thought a heating pad would soothe them. Unfortunately, it was an old and faulty heating pad, and over the course of the night it slipped down to my shin and remained there until morning. I didn't notice I'd been burned until I put my socks on and my fingers rubbed past the raw spot. That afternoon a huge blister formed, and by the time I was getting ready for bed, it had popped. I left it alone, thinking it would heal, but over time it became inflamed, red, sore, and puffy around its edges. It hurt to touch, so I threw a Band-Aid on it and hoped for the best, but eventually I had trouble walking because the pain was so bad.

I went to the emergency room, where they cleaned it and looked at it. As it turns out, the wound was ulcerated. The ulcer was on the bone, and until the ulcer came up to the surface, it wouldn't heal. I would have to keep peeling off the white scab that kept trying to form, and clean the wound. Eventually the ulcer reached the surface, and a scab formed. Although there's a small scar there now, there's no remaining pain. It has healed.

I often think of that wound and the lesson it taught me. I touch the scar and can think of a thousand hurts that needed to heal in just that way before the scab could form. You don't mind a scar so much if the pain is gone.

When I woke up on January 31, I went about my normal morning routine with Tim, but before he had even left for work, I had to lie down again. I didn't feel right; although I couldn't name the problem, I thought if I just rested, I'd be okay. By one o'clock that afternoon, I was worried. I hadn't felt the baby moving for a couple of hours, despite trying to wake him up with sugary drinks and chocolate, and even throwing in some very loud U2 music for him to listen to. Nothing was working, and around two o'clock in the afternoon, I began to cramp.

I phoned the church, but Tim was in a meeting, and I didn't know if this would classify as an emergency or not. In hindsight, that really is as stupid as it sounds. I had begun to feel like a drama queen, begging for attention and being rushed off to hospital every few days. As I put this down on paper, though, I see again the stupidity of those thoughts, but reality and stupidity are often closely knitted together. I left a message asking that he call me as soon as he could, and then I sat and waited with the phone in my hand. I had phoned twice more before the receptionist finally asked if everything was okay. I quietly admitted that I thought it might be an emergency and that I would need to interrupt the meeting. Tim was on the phone within minutes. He had the car at the office, so he felt it would be faster if I took a cab to the hospital, and he would meet me there.

Having a plan helped, so I got up, got my coat from the closet, and my purse from the hook, and called the cab company. The wait for the cab was probably one of the longest of my life. When he finally got to the house, I locked the door and calmly waddled to the car. I explained that while this wasn't an urgent situation, I was indeed pregnant and needed to get to the hospital in the timeliest manner he could manage. I smiled when he simply responded with "Oh my God!" and stepped on the gas. I had to reiterate a few times on the drive that I wasn't in labour and he didn't need to break laws to get us there. He almost didn't want to take my money; he was so busy trying to get me out of his cab that I had to remind him that I owed him twenty bucks.

I got into the hospital and went to labour and delivery on the seventh floor. I've since wondered why they make pregnant women, who are often in pain, go all the way to the seventh floor. I understand that the first floor needs to be the ER, but why not have maternity on the second floor? Why do we need to go to the seventh floor? That's a lot of floors when you're cramping and scared or, worse, in active labour!

When I finally reached the triage area, they informed me that I needed to get admitted, which happened on the first floor. I could have cried, and while I don't remember it very well, I think I might have done so in the privacy of the long elevator ride back down to the first floor. As I turned the corner toward admitting, I saw Tim standing there waiting for me. I can't tell you how wonderful it was to see him standing in front of me, offering his arms to me. Never have I felt so safe, never has it taken so much courage to leave that safe place. The funny part (funny as in not funny at all) is that it was around this time that the cramps stopped and I began to feel very silly. Had I dragged Tim out of a meeting, worked myself up to a frenzy, and almost gotten a cabbie arrested for reckless driving for nothing? Would the doctors look at me and see a panicky new mother-to-be and dismiss me as silly? I was hoping this would be the case, but at the same time I felt very dramatic and stupid.

We were admitted anyway and made the long trek back up to the seventh floor. The triage nurse came in and hooked me up to a monitor and then quickly ordered an ultrasound machine to be brought to my bed. They did a scan and then called in the doctor. It wasn't our usual doctor; this one's name was Doctor K., and he seemed much more uptight. He appeared to think things were bad, and tension almost radiated off him in a way I could physically feel. He had me come to another machine so that they could have a better look. He said it didn't look good, and that they were going to have to take the baby. The flow on the cord was going backwards, and the baby was starving because the placenta was failing him. I looked at Tim in shock. This was unreal. We'd had an ultrasound the day before, and it hadn't revealed anything wrong. What had happened? Had I moved weirdly in the night? Did I eat something that caused this? Did I do this? Was my unfriendly womb trying to evict my son?

This was my first interaction with Dr. K. Now that I know him, ever since he started coming to our old church, I realize he isn't normally so uptight, but my situation called for it. At the time, though, it made me nervous. I wanted calm Dr. R. back to give his soothing advice. I wanted to hear his relaxed "no worries." If he couldn't say that but instead agreed with Dr. K., then I would agree to the procedure.

Before I could even articulate my wish, Dr. R. came in. He'd been on his way home when word came to him that we were back. After speaking with Dr. K. and viewing the images himself, he agreed. Joshua wanted to join us now, and we couldn't wait. The surgery was going to happen regardless of the outcome; Joshua would be born that night.

Tim made phone calls to our parents while I sat paralyzed with fear, thinking about the doctors who'd said that he couldn't come early. All the pediatricians had agreed that, with Joshua's heart problems, he wouldn't survive an early birth. So what would this mean for us? If Dr. R. was no longer calm, what did it mean for Joshua? People were surrounding me, prepping me for surgery and asking questions about when I had eaten last and what allergies I had. After he called our parents, Tim was stuck out of the way at the foot of the bed. But when he saw my fear, he got up and pushed past nurses, saying, "Let me get to my wife; she's scared." I've had a million moments in our marriage when I've felt safe and loved, but this one stands out so clearly to me. He knew what I needed, and he was going to slay dragons to get to my side to be there and offer his safety and comfort.

A pediatrician came in and started talking about risks. With his heart condition, Josh's chances of survival were low, if he had any to begin with. All I could think about was the doctor who had warned me to bring a camera when the baby was born, because it would most likely be my one chance to have a photo of my son. My heart filled with panic. I hadn't brought a camera. I needed a camera. It's amazing what happens in the face of fear, the things you think about. They gave Tim the consent forms to sign and started to wheel me away, but Tim stopped them and asked for a moment to pray with me. I don't remember the words of the prayer, but I do remember feeling peace. This was it, our moment of truth. Miracle or no miracle, we would find out tonight.

FIVE

"Have I not commanded you? Be strong and courageous!
Do not tremble or be dismayed, for the Lord your God
is with you wherever you go."
~Joshua 1:9~

TIM SIGNED THE CONSENT FORM. THEY WERE WHEELING ME FROM THE room when the pediatrician said to Tim, "Prepare yourselves that he will probably die." I had heard it before, and it had registered. More of the ulcer rising to the surface, waiting to be pulled off again. Would we ever be free of that festering ulcer? Would they ever just stop with the dire threats and predictions? Couldn't they just once say, "We're going to do our very best to see that your son lives tonight"? Would that be so difficult?

Tim wasn't allowed in the room until I'd been given the epidural and was totally prepped for surgery; in fact, they had already made the first cut when he was finally allowed to come and stand beside my head. He spoke to me, words I can't remember but which soothed me at the time. He walked me through what was happening and told me that everything would be okay. I have no clear memory of the surgery. What I do remember has been pieced together by Tim and the doctors and some foggy snapshots of my own.

The doctors were working on me when they started to say things like "Oh my goodness!" or "Does someone have a camera?" or "This is amazing." Everyone was so busy looking at my insides and the baby resting there, they forgot that I couldn't see what was happening. It's entirely possible that they just plain forgot about me in general. Even Tim was so busy looking over the sheet that it was the anesthesiologist who finally explained it all to me. The baby had wrapped the cord around his leg eight times. They were taking photos because it was so rare that in Dr. K.'s entire career (he is a placenta specialist), he had never seen it. This was to be a first of many rare things that Joshua has become known for. He's one of those one in a million kids. I found out later that those pictures have been submitted to medical journals, so some med student out there will one day see my insides and heaven knows what else. Lovely thought, right? My fifteen minutes of fame, I guess.

I clearly remember when they pulled Joshua from my body. There was tugging, and then the pop as he left me. My unfriendly womb had been evacuated, and I felt hollow, empty, and frightened. I saw him, but only briefly as they rushed him to another room. I remember the nurse turning to show him to me as she rushed him from the room, and I remember his dark eyes, open and looking at me, haunting me with a look that seemed to ask for help. He was blue and tiny, and I hadn't heard him cry, although Tim says that he heard him in the other room.

I was taken to recovery and was so cold, I couldn't stop the shaking. I was also very confused. Nothing seemed to make any sense. There were gaps in time, giant holes that I fell into and cannot remember. Ask most mothers and they'll be able to tell you blow-by-blow details of the birth of their child, especially when it's the first. This is something I can't do, and it left me feeling empty, sad, and not at all what I had imagined back on July 1 when I learned of his existence.

My mother and Tim stood with me, trying to calm and reassure me, but all I wanted to know was when I could hold him, when I could see him. The separation was so swift, so brutal, and I felt alone and empty. We had been together for eight months, and because of the situation, I was hyper-aware of all his changes, from wake to sleep. I was aware of his kicks and his hiccups; just knowing he was present inside of me brought comfort. There had been no gradual movement toward birth; we hadn't laboured long to achieve this separation. He had been cut from me before his time and certainly before I was ready to let him go. And now I didn't know where he was. I couldn't feel him, and I didn't know if he was going to live. At that point, I didn't even know if he was still breathing. Looking back on that night, all I see is a foggy darkness that was not the birth of my son but the night they took him out of me.

When a child is born, the family comes to visit. They bring flowers and balloons. The doctors and nurses say "It's a boy," followed by congratulations. You're given a little person, wrapped in a soft blue blanket, and he nuzzles into you and falls asleep, or maybe he's hungry and starts to suckle you right away. He is born. You are a mother, and he is your son. That bond is there, and you begin the greatest adventure. It was different for us, and I grieved that for a long time before learning to let it go.

I lay in my bed, asking for the thousandth time when I would see him, when I would be able to just look at him, to hold him. They finally allowed me to see him, but it was not what I had thought it would be. He was blue; he was naked, save for a diaper. I didn't know diapers came that small, and his tiny little body was covered with tubes and IVs. The only space on his body that I could touch without disturbing the wires and tubes was a small space on his forehead, just above his tiny little nose. Holding him was out of the question, and it made my arms ache. I kept saying, "He's going to be cold," but I don't think anyone heard me, or maybe I didn't speak my thoughts. I don't remember. I remember he looked at me; those dark eyes stared up at me, and I knew that he knew me. It seemed I could see all the pain and fear in those little eyes, and my heart broke. Wasn't it my job to protect him from pain? Was I already, just hours into motherhood, failing him?

I try to imagine what it must be like for such a little life to be taken from the only thing he has ever known, a place that is safe and warm and comforting, and to be placed into a loud, bright, cold place where they hurt you and prod at you and stick you with needles and tubes and force things down your throat. I felt sick with these thoughts, but I couldn't share them, couldn't voice my thoughts, because once I did, they would be real, and I couldn't handle any more reality.

I was only allowed a few minutes with him before they took me back to the recovery room to wait—for what, I have no idea. All I wanted was to be with him. Nothing was going to make this okay, and no one could help. Not even God.

Several years ago, I lived in a tiny village in the Austrian Alps. At night it was so dark, you couldn't see the road in front of you. During a particularly hard point in life, I was walking home on one such dark night. I kept missing steps and nearly fell a number of times. At one point I stopped to catch my footing and couldn't help but look up. When I did, I was amazed at what I saw—a thousand, or maybe even a million, pinpricks of light, brilliant stars, scattered across the dark night sky, lighting up the heavens. Had it not been so dark, had I not looked up, I would have missed the stars. Life can throw curve balls, the sunlight can't always shine, there are times when darkness inevitably comes, but I have tried to look up since that time in the mountains of Austria, and I have tried to see the stars. In every dark time, you can see the blessings that you're given, the moments when God has reached out and touched your life through someone else or through his own peace and comfort; it's just not always the easiest thing to see, and sometimes we're so focused on finding our footing, we don't look up.

Lying there in the recovery room that night, I looked up and saw stars, little moments of blessing mixed into the fog of the dark nights that consumed us. Things that seemed so horrific at the time later proved to be part of the larger plan that would see Joshua live through that birth. There was a time when I bemoaned even knowing about the possibility of heart defects. I wanted to stay in ignorance and enjoy pregnancy like any other woman, but what would have happened had I not known? He would have been born at thirty weeks, on January 1, 2008, and we would have buried him the same week. It was a star in the night sky. Had that whole episode on January 1 not happened, I wouldn't have had the shot of steroids that would make Joshua's lungs stronger in case of early delivery, and he wouldn't have survived the birth. Had we not known that there were possible complications causing him to not move within the womb, I wouldn't have been afraid that Thursday. Had those cramps not come, I wouldn't have gone to the hospital as quickly as I did, and

Joshua would have been a stillbirth. God is my north star in the night sky, and when it's dark, I must remind myself to stop and look up.

While I was in recovery that night, a nurse said to me, "It's so good that you came in when you did; you saved your son's life." I remember telling her that she was wrong, that God had done it. I remember her looking at me with a little smile that seemed to say, "The poor girl had too much of the pain medication" (which, given the lack of memory, is probably slightly true, and I wasn't complaining). The stars aren't always easy to see; sometimes light pollution and clouds block them from view, but they are there, nonetheless.

That night Tim had to go to SickKids to be with Josh, sign the consent, and just be near him. I was glad he was there; I didn't want to think of Joshua alone in an entirely different hospital from me. The reality of that meant that I was alone, emotional, and hormonal. I couldn't sleep, I was in pain, and I could hear the babies in the other rooms crying. I wanted to hear my baby cry. I wanted to comfort him like the other mothers were doing in the bed and rooms beside me.

My room was sparse, with only my jacket from the night before and a magazine that had been left by another patient. There were no decorations, no flowers or balloons to signify the fact that we'd welcomed our son into the world that night. There was no joyful card to wish us well on the journey of parenthood. It was just an empty room, and my body was just as empty. The only person who visited me in that hospital room was Tim, because our parents had staked their claim in the CCCU (Cardiac Critical Care Unit) waiting room at SickKids, where I was wheeled through a tunnel under the hospital each morning and night by Tim and once by a nurse, whom I'd begged to take me to visit with Joshua when Tim was running late one morning. Mt. Sinai ended up calling the CCCU waiting room to find me so that they could discharge me and free up my unused bed. So I left, with care instructions and medication, and took my place in the waiting room just a hallway away from Joshua's bed.

It wasn't until he was three days old that Joshua received his first welcome balloons. To me, those balloons were so significant, a sign that this was real, that I had a son who was alive, who was worth celebrating, and people other than me loved him. He was a reason for joy. While the situation wasn't ideal, because he was sick and things didn't look all that great for him, that would never alter the fact that he lived. No one really understood how much it meant to me. I'm not sure they even understand now. I didn't want to mourn him, not when he was alive! I wanted to celebrate him and rejoice that he was here at all. That alone was a miracle worth buying balloons and stuffed bears for!

The hardest part of those first days of motherhood was the ache inside to hold him, to have his skin touching mine, to feel him move, to know his warmth, to be close to him again. My biggest fear was that he wouldn't be able to bond with me. I couldn't feed him, and I couldn't hold him. The only thing I could do for my child was change his diaper, and even then I had to fight through a maze of tubes and wires to maneuvre a clean change.

The doctors said things that I didn't understand; it seemed to me that they were doing nothing. Joshua was hooked up to all these machines, including life support, yet no one would do anything to help him. He needed the balloon dilatation that they had told us about way back at the beginning of this nightmare, but every day there was some reason why they couldn't do it. When they tried to explain why, the explanation was so scientific, I didn't understand. Tim tried to explain it to me, but all I could really hear was that it wasn't going to happen today. One more day of not holding him; one more day of watching him just lie there, no closer to health than the day before.

He'd been given so many medications, he was swollen to double his actual size. His tummy swelled so much that it literally ripped the skin. That tear now forever marks him; it was his very first scar. His head was so full of fluid that his ear became deformed and misshapen. When I asked his nurse about this, he simply informed me about the wonders of plastic surgery. I felt silly caring about aesthetics when his life was still in the balance, but my stomach felt sick, nonetheless. His forehead was still the only place we could touch. We still had not heard his cry, and I'd only seen his eyes on the night they took him. I missed him; he was so still. I hadn't known him long, but I had lain awake so many nights feeling him kick at me, that now, seeing him so still, made me miss him.

SIX

At the castle in Austria there's a small chapel dating back to the 1500s. It was well used, always very cold, but so pretty and quiet. The chapel is tucked into the wall of the castle, perched above the gatehouse and safely up from the driveway. There's a window at the top of the chapel wall, actually more of a slit, just enough to let in the cold night air as well as the light of the stars. One very cold and dark night the chapel was empty, so I went in. I needed a quiet place to pray for a moment, so I sat on the bench behind the door. If anyone looked in, they wouldn't see me and try to talk. The chapel was dark, and the moonlight coming through the slit window revealed the dusty air in a streak of light that pierced the darkness. I sat there, just needing to hide for a while in God's presence. I sat there waiting for a whisper. As the moonlight danced on the ceiling through that slit window, the words of a hymn came to mind:

Great is Thy faithfulness, O God my Father!
There is no shadow of turning with Thee;

Thou changest not, Thy compassions, they fail not:
As Thou hast been Thou forever wilt be.
Great is Thy faithfulness! Great is Thy faithfulness!
Morning by morning new mercies I see;
All I have needed Thy hand hath provided—
Great is Thy faithfulness, Lord, unto me!
Summer and winter, and springtime and harvest,
Sun, moon and stars in their courses above,
Join with all nature in manifold witness
To Thy great faithfulness, mercy and love.
Pardon for sin and a peace that endureth,
Thine own dear presence to cheer and to guide,
Strength for today and bright hope for tomorrow—
Blessings all mine, with ten thousand beside![2]

In that moment, I became aware of something more clearly than I'd ever been aware of anything in my life. I loved God. For the first time in my life, I could say it and mean it. It was no longer going to be a relationship where I took love and didn't return it. I loved him, and I wanted to know everything I could about him. He was enough for me; his faithfulness had been new every morning, his mercies fresh like dew every day. Despite how I had acted, withholding love and rejecting him, he had shed tears for me and never given up on me. He had never stopped pursuing me, loving me. It was a love I had been searching for my entire life, right there in front of me, and I finally saw it with new eyes. I finally understood that he and he alone was what I'd been looking for. That night in the chapel I became a new person. It was the night I began to heal from old wounds, the night my life changed and I charted a new course.

Now, sitting in the CCCU and waiting for Joshua's catheterization, I felt that urge to get close to God again, to feel his embrace, to have him near me. I found myself taking up daily residence in the hospital chapel, begging God to make it okay, reminding him that he had promised

[2] Thomas O. Chisholm, "Great Is Thy Faithfulness," (No.21) in *Living Praise Hymnal* (Grand Rapids, MI: Zondervan, 1977).

me that he would do the impossible. The more I prayed, the quieter he became. The chapel was empty, and it felt like God hadn't shown up. All around me people were telling me that they were praying for Joshua. "Praying for you" became a substitute for "talk to you later." What I hated most was people telling me just to have faith and that everything would be fine if I just had faith. Well, guess what? It wasn't fine, it wasn't going to be fine, and I had faith, albeit tested. More seeds of anger and frustration took root, unnoticed by me.

While I realize that other people were affected by Josh's illness, I can't talk for them. Tim struggled with all of this in his own way. He loves Joshua as much as I do, and watching his son go through that pain and suffering was difficult for him as well. He suffered spiritually, agonizing over the big theological questions, particularly about where God was in the midst of this pain. On top of that, Tim had the additional burden of caring for me, since I had undergone major surgery and was coping with all the normal hormonal changes that happen when you have a child. Our parents struggled. It wasn't just their grandchild but their children who were hurting, and they couldn't fix it. We were all helpless in the face of this crisis; not one of us could control the outcome of one of the most critical things we've ever gone through. No one went without suffering.

And that's also what made me angry and resentful—that Tim and I needed to comfort others in this. We needed support, yet as events unfolded, we were the ones who had to answer questions and offer words of hope and comfort. I desperately wanted someone to explain this to me, to come alongside and comfort me, to envelope Tim in his or her arms and allow him for once to lean on someone for the strength he was losing by giving it to me.

When Joshua was first diagnosed, I asked our pastor and Tim's boss to come to our home and pray with us. He came by first thing that morning, and after listening to our story, he simply blurted out an emphatic expletive that shook me to the core. As shocking or un-Christian as some might think that sounds, it was about the sweetest and most comforting thing I heard through the entire process. No other word described how I felt. He didn't offer false hope or platitudes, he didn't question what sin we must have committed in the past to lead us to this place, and he didn't offer to pray and then pat us on the back and wish us well. No, he took the dirt on his hands as he waded through the muddy water with us. He joined us in our pain and anxiety.

At one point (much later in our journey) I got an email from a friend in Poland. She and her husband were going through a similar situation. Her little girl was facing a heart operation, and she asked me how I managed. I answered her questions as well as I could, but the exchange raised many things that I wanted people to know and understand, so I wrote this blog post:

> *Sit with me in the moment, allow me to run the gamut of my emotions, let me rage, let me vent, let me cry, let me even feel sorry for myself once in a while! Then, after you have allowed for all of that, you can say "I'm sorry." Not for the life we created, not for the child who is ill, but for the pain they suffer, for the fear that we are feeling, for the grief that we feel.*
> *~ Through the Lens of Motherhood ~*

It was in essence the very thing that our pastor allowed us to do. He recognized that this was a moment we needed to sit in for a while. We needed to grieve and have the permission to do just that.

There was a thirteen-year-old young man with cancer in the ICU at the same time that we were waiting for Josh's surgery. His mother, I'll call her Sarah, was one of the women camped out with me daily in the CCCU, because her son was dying. She was Sikh, and she was alone most days. We didn't talk too much. We each had our own thoughts and things that we needed to do. Her son needed her, and mine needed me. However, during shift change twice a day when we were unable to be in our sons' rooms, we would sit on a couch together and talk about what had brought us to this point.

In the CCCU, you track time differently than you do in the outside world. You measure time not by day but by hour. You can't count on anything more than what is real in that moment. Right now might look hopeless, but in five minutes it could all change. If Joshua was doing well right now, it was something to be celebrated. If he was doing poorly, you had to hang on until the next moment, because maybe that would be a better one. Each week consisted of this swinging pendulum—a good day, then a bad day. Each day was a journey through the highest of highs and the lowest of lows. Each day you were stuck in a time warp where the outside world didn't exist, and the only person you really wanted to hear from was the doctor.

It still amazes me how so many of the things that I used to consider major life problems became nothing once I found myself in the reality of the CCCU. My life, while filled with little dramas along the way, had been easy until those moments. No problem before or since will ever really compare; the hard part is to remember to not take it for granted. I discovered during those weeks that suffering is yours alone. What hurts me, what worries me, may be nothing compared to what worries someone else. That lesson has served me well when listening to someone else's pain or fears. I can't count the times when someone has shared something with me about their own suffering and then quickly added, "But it's nothing compared to what you've gone through." It makes me sad to hear this, because suffering is just that—suffering. No one escapes it, and no one can compare it. We feel what we feel, we grieve how we grieve, and we worry about what we worry about. That's life. I'd rather hear about someone else's pain and be able to offer comfort than be held at bay because someone thinks his or her suffering is somehow less than mine. We are made for community so that when the storms hit, we have someone to help us keep our heads above water; it doesn't matter how deep that water is or how good a swimmer we are.

Sarah was a quiet woman. She didn't talk much to anyone, and she didn't have anyone who came and spent time with her in the hospital. Yet when I watched her, I saw her quiet strength. She would read her Granth (the Sikh scriptures) whenever she wasn't either sleeping or sitting with her son, and I suspect she read it when he slept as well. I don't believe in her prophets, but I believe in her faith. Where was my Bible? It wasn't in the CCCU waiting room.

When the doctors told her that the end was very near, we started to see her family and friends show up. Tim and I were so impressed with how they grieved with her; it was like a sitting Shiva. They came in, two or three together, sat beside her, and said nothing. They responded only if she spoke. They didn't ask questions or offer false comfort. They just sat with her while she read or prayed or cried or talked. For two days this went on. She wasn't left alone during this period; people came in shifts, an hour here or a few hours there. Always just sitting beside her, holding her hand through her grief but allowing her to guide that grief, allowing her to guide their comfort. It was beautiful to see, and it left a deep impression on me as I sat witness to it.

Her son didn't die. He lived and got stronger. I was given reports about how he was gaining weight, going back to school, thriving. That period of mourning was over for Sarah. She was given more time— how much time, I don't know. But should any new tragedy unfold in their lives, I know she'll have a support system that amazes me and will comfort her. If only we could all support each other like that, if only we didn't feel the need to fill grief and silence or tears with words that are often just filler and forgotten shortly after spoken.

SEVEN

WHEN JOSHUA TURNED SIX DAYS OLD, WE FINALLY GOT THE GO-AHEAD for the catheterization. I was elated! This is what we'd been waiting for, the hope we were hanging on for, what we'd been courageous and strong for. This was the beginning of the end of our suffering. The fetal echo doctor had told us that the balloon catheterization would be the cure for him, that he'd be fine once it was over, and we'd be able to take him home soon after. On February 6, 2008, they took Joshua into the catheterization lab on the fourth floor in the old part of the SickKids Hospital. The area looked like a spaceship, with giant lava lamps and walls that looked like moon rocks. A little boy's dream playground.

Prior to being born, you have what's called an ASD, a small hole between the two ventricles through which the blood flows. Since you aren't breathing, there's no need for the blood to go through the lungs. It can be pumped directly from right to left without being filtered. Usually that hole closes just days after birth. In Joshua's case, medication was given to prevent that hole from closing, because his pulmonary valve didn't exist. He needed that hole, or the blood would have nowhere to go. It wasn't ideal; his oxygen levels were in the 60s and 70s when they should have been 98–100. There was talk about closing the hole when he was old enough and strong enough to tolerate the surgery, around one year or even two depending on how his heart handled the balloon catheterization. We needed to resolve the issue of this pulmonary valve. The right ventricle was working so hard, it was building up too much muscle mass, which meant the space for blood to flow was growing smaller. Ultimately, we were trying to prevent heart failure while holding off on invasive surgery or procedures until he was bigger and stronger.

Dr. B. (the catheterization specialist) explained what the procedure would look like and how they would take care of things like pain management or blood thinning to avoid a stroke. All fairly basic pre-surgery stuff, so we signed the consent and began the wait. We didn't wait long.

When the procedure was over and Joshua was taken back to the CCCU to recover, the doctor came to tell us that the procedure had been a success. He even had an X-ray-type photo of Joshua's heart and the pulmonary valve so we could better understand what had taken place behind closed doors that day. I walked back down to the CCCU waiting room and couldn't speak; I saw my mom and just broke down. The relief, the weight that had lifted, the end of trying to be strong was finally too much. The good news had been my release valve, and all I could do was cry in my mother's arms and let her comfort me.

Now the road to recovery could begin. We sat at his bedside for hours; some of those hours were good, some not so good. Talk of weaning him off oxygen would get our hopes up, while a dip in his saturation levels would mean more oxygen and we'd be on the emotional roller coaster again. Up and down it went, for days on end. Tim and I were exhausted, full of crappy food, and desperate to hold our baby boy, to cuddle him for just a minute. I craved the times the nurse changed his sheet in the morning, because it meant I could lift him briefly while she pulled the old sheet out and put the new sheet in. It was the smallest of moments, but it made my ache seem a little less acute.

One night, Tim was able to get me to go home with him. I needed a shower, fresh clothes, and sleep. We lay in bed whispering into the night about how much we wished for simple things, like seeing his eyes open, or getting a response when we touched him— anything would be better than seeing him so lifeless, swollen, and still. We prayed until sleep claimed us.

The next morning, we were back in the CCCU before shift change. I didn't want Joshua to think that we hadn't been there, that we had left him. The nurse was adjusting his meds when we came into the room, and we asked her about his night. As soon as he heard our voices, his eyes opened and he looked at us for the first time since the night he was born two weeks before. We scooted to the bed, each of us taking one tiny finger, and in the same moment, he squeezed our fingers back. Tim and I looked at each other, tears falling; this was not only an answer to our prayers of the night before but a gift of hope from God. Looking back, that was the moment that stands out so clearly; that was our "birth" moment.

Not long after this event, we were told that we'd be moving up to 4D. This is where you go when you graduate from CCCU. CCCU is 1:1 nurse-to-patient ratio, and it's the ICU of the cardiology department. A step-down unit has a 1:2 nurse-to-patient ratio, but the graduation that really matters is going to 4D. It's the place cardiac families long for, the Olympic gold, so to speak, as it's the cardiology ward where you have a private room with your child, and the nurse-to-patient ratio is 1:4. This is where you can be a parent again, or for the very first time, like us. You can get a little sleep, and when you do wake up, it's because your child is crying and needs you to feed or change them. You finally get to hold your sweet little baby for the first time and give him the love you've been aching to give. The nurses there talk about normal things, like breast-feeding issues and weight gain. Because Joshua was so small and underweight, we learned about skin-to-skin contact. Even on the wakeful nights, the fear and dread don't hang over you like before—the fear that you'll be called to his bedside with news that his heart isn't responding, or that his O2 levels are bad. On 4D, your child is beside you, living and breathing, and the end game is to get you home.

We got to 4D at the end of Joshua's second week. I was able to spend the night with him and feed him, though not from the breast yet. But

I got to be his mother. That's where I heard him cry for the first time. He couldn't cry before because he'd had so many tubes in his throat; his face would scrunch up in pain, but no sound would come out, just silent cries. On 4D I heard his cry, as did everyone else, I'm afraid. It was loud and demanding and strong. Even so, we had to fight for him many times on 4D. They'd put him on oxygen when his SATS (blood saturation levels, which is the measurement of oxygen in the blood) were too low. Those numbers are absolutely vital, and you tend to stare at the monitors for hours watching them, hoping for an increase, and stomach flipping when they dip slightly. When that would happen, he'd take a step backwards as far as weaning off oxygen. They woke us every hour, which resulted in me having difficulty producing enough milk, so he wasn't gaining weight, and we couldn't take out the feeding tube.

He was so small, just four pounds. His body temperature was difficult to maintain, so I had to keep him wrapped tightly, but the nurses were constantly unwrapping him to check this or that. He was put into an incubator, where he screamed for hours until his saturation levels dipped to dangerous lows. I finally convinced them to let me try to keep him warm with the blankets, only unwrapping him when necessary and doing everything they needed at the same time so that we didn't have to unwrap him again for quite a while.

I felt like a real mother for the first time, and when the treatment worked, he was able to maintain his own body heat without being stuck in an incubator. I had fought for my son, and he was a step ahead because of it. It gave Tim and me courage to stand up for him in other areas as well. We noticed that the oxygen had slipped out of his nose one day; we also noted that his levels were okay (at least they were at a place the doctor would tolerate), so we waited and didn't tell anyone. It wasn't fixed for an hour, but nothing changed; his SATS had remained stable. We didn't try to kill our son, and we weren't being irresponsible. We were only trying to fight on his behalf, to help wean him off oxygen. Had his levels dipped, we would have simply put the nose prongs back in. We were watching him carefully.

Some people were angry with us. They thought we didn't know what was best, but ultimately it was the doctor's opinion that mattered, and she was pleased with the results. He was breathing on his own, his colour was okay, and though not perfect, his saturation levels were at a place she would tolerate until he was old enough to have something done about them.

By the next day, I had him weaned from the feeding tube to a bottle, which silently broke my heart because it meant that he would likely never take the breast. But it also meant there was a better chance of having him gain weight, and that ultimately mattered more. No one thinks of these little details when they think of having a child. You get pregnant and you decide to either breastfeed or bottle-feed. It's a given that it will be your choice, and the pressure to do the "natural thing," which translates into the "best thing," is unreal. If you aren't breastfeeding, you're judged. I had wanted to breastfeed my child, dreamed about the intimacy of it, and was deeply saddened that it couldn't happen. No one knew that, though, when they saw me bottle-feeding my baby, just as no one knows the real reasons many people do things we don't agree with.

The first time Joshua was wireless, I took him for a walk down the hall. I showed him the window so that he could feel the sunlight on his face, and I sat with him anywhere but our room, because I wanted him to begin enjoying the world outside the hospital. I wanted him home, and to do that he would need to fight. It didn't take him long. Our doctor began to listen to us differently after we had weaned him off the oxygen, and on Sunday, February 17, at 9:00 a.m. when she did her rounds, I asked if I could take him home, explaining that if he were home I would be better rested and could produce more milk. I also suggested that he would be better rested as well. She listened and heard me, then nodded her head. Because we lived so close, she agreed to sign the discharge papers.

When Joshua left the hospital that day, he weighed only 4 lbs. 4 oz. He was so small, I had to dress him in four outfits piled one on top of the other so that he would be big enough to fit into his car seat. She released us with the promise that we would get him weighed every day until we saw her again the following week. Never have I felt such elation! My baby was coming home to the nursery that no one had thought he would use. His pain, and ours, had not been in vain.

EIGHT

THE JOY THAT FILLED OUR HEARTS WHEN WE STEPPED OUTSIDE WITH our son beside us, the drive home where we sat in happy silence, the phone call to my parents to tell them he was home, was all part of such a wonderful moment in our lives. We felt giddy with the relief; the worst was over, and now it was time to rejoice and recover.

We celebrated that night. We made dinner, and my parents and grandfather brought a cake with "Welcome home, Joshua" written across it. All of us sat in wonder watching him breathe, watching him sleep unattached to tubes or wires. After my parents left, we enjoyed snuggles, feedings, and his first bath and change. Projectile poop and pee that arced to the ceiling left us amazed and joyful. We were the exhausted parents of this little one, and we reveled in the miracle of finally being able to care for him.

One moment stands out in particular. I woke up early to feed Joshua. We were tired. We were always tired, but this time Tim got up to keep me company and enjoy the moment. He read to me while I fed Joshua, and I loved him all the more for it. His father's heart was finally allowed free rein to express all his love for his son because of the hope that bringing Joshua home had stirred in him. Tim would wake at every sound, listening to Joshua breathe, ensuring that he was still breathing. He fed him, changed him, and cared for him. He held him for hours and slept beside him during naps. It was beautiful to watch, and as a new mother and wife, I was witnessing the love that is entwined in both those roles. Tim expressed the pride he felt in Joshua's will to live by frequently saying "That's my boy." I felt so blessed by God to see my husband bloom into fatherhood so easily, to watch him care for Joshua and for me so tenderly. In spite of the sleep deprivation, those first weeks with Joshua home were restful in the peace that came from having answers and knowing that the major struggle was over.

With the initial trauma behind us, we began to settle into life as new parents, which as any new parent knows, means exhaustion. The first few weeks were the hardest as we adjusted to the role made more challenging because of Joshua's special needs. It was wonderful that he started to gain weight, but he cried all the time, and when he got too upset, he'd turn blue because his saturation levels would drop. We couldn't just let him cry it out, which meant I was up all night with him.

They tell you that you need to nap while he naps, but whoever "they" are have forgotten about housework, laundry, work, and the marriage you're trying to hold together and enjoy. By Easter of 2008, we were beyond tired. At one point it had been a full forty-eight hours of crying, and Tim and I were at the end of our collective rope. We argued a lot, both of us felt harder done by than the other, both of us were still recovering emotionally from the roller coaster of the last few months, and both of us were in desperate need of sleep. On the Monday of Holy Week (the Monday before Easter), we finally decided to call for help. We arrived at my parents' door, handed the baby to my mom, and went to her bed for a good long nap.

Tim had Easter services coming up that week and needed rest, and since I knew he'd be busy, we decided that I would stay with my mom to get some help and rest. Finally, on the Saturday after Good Friday, a nurse practitioner friend from the States who was visiting suggested that Joshua might have a milk allergy, so we went out and bought soy formula as soon as we could. Joshua slept well that night, and the crying that never seemed to end just as suddenly stopped.

My unfriendly womb had taken over my unfriendly breasts. I didn't have the body to mother a child, and it was a painful realization, a confirmation of my worst fear—I really was a total failure. There are expectations to being a woman, a mother specifically, that men don't experience. Breastfeeding is one. If you don't breastfeed, other mothers silently and not so silently judge you. I remember feeding Joshua once through a bottle (pumped milk), and a mother of two came up and asked why I wasn't breastfeeding "that baby." The hurt hit first, then the anger, but ultimately it was the hurt that won out. She had touched a nerve. I had so wanted to breastfeed Joshua and bond with him that way. Losing out on that experience was one of the things I grieved the most. I felt that I had failed him. A button was pushed every time someone said something like that, and it reminded me that I was failing at the most important thing I desperately wanted to do. I began to wonder if guilt wasn't more what motherhood was about, clinging like a plague and generating fear and anxiety. These were new feelings for me, as I'd always been the laid-back, easy going one. I'd always been the fearless, strong, fun-loving woman, but I could also feel changes afoot. Either I had no emotional strength at that point to deal with them, or I had no time to really dig in to explore these new feelings, but I pushed the feelings down where they would fester for some years.

I also wasn't talking to God during this period of time. It wasn't a deliberate turning away from him … more like both of us being quiet. Today, many years later, I realize that the hiding was one-sided and resided with me alone, but at the time I was so tired, I didn't even notice it happening. By the time I did notice it, I had nothing to say. I was left numb from the trauma of the year, and I was unable to express anything, even though I could still feel awe at God's mighty hand, amazement at the many blessings, wonderment at those little stars that filled our night sky. I just had no words to share my deepest fears, my darkest doubts, and no words to tell him how thankful or lonely I was. My lack of words made me feel so far from him, so alone and lost from his sight.

I remember sitting on the glasshouse wall of the castle in Austria and wishing that one day I would have the love of a good man, someone who could really love me and truly know me. It was a wish, but as it floated on the breeze God heard it, and years later I look at Tim and know that God heard me that day. I never intended it as a prayer, but I've learned that prayer doesn't always have to be intentional. God knows us; he knows our thoughts, hurts, and deepest unspoken desires, and he loves us. Whether or not we pray with intention doesn't change any of that. God hears us and he answers us. I wasn't talking to him, but he was there, listening to me. I had just forgotten that. In my self-pity and self-centred human way, I'd taken his perceived silence as his absence, and it hurt more deeply than I realized. It remained that way for quite some time.

At this point, Joshua was growing in so many ways. He got chubby on the soymilk, and soon his wrists disappeared into his folds of fat in the cute way only babies can get away with. Dimples on his elbows appeared, and before long they showed up on his cheeks. His cheeky personality started to form too!

NINE

IT WAS AROUND THIS TIME THAT WE HAD A ROUTINE FOLLOW-UP cardiology appointment at SickKids. Other parents had told us that the follow-up is just a routine thing, and usually you get told to come back in a year. So when we took Joshua to the hospital that day, we weren't prepared for the news we got. The hole in the valve they'd created with the balloon dilation had shrunk and wasn't working properly, and the muscle build-up of the ventricle was large enough to cause the atrium to shrink as well. A second catheterization was required. Tim and I were in shock; we'd thought he was cured … or at least that the major stuff was over.

The procedure was set for the following week. On Thursday, April 24, just four days before we were to celebrate our first anniversary in New York City, we took him to the hospital, feeling anxious and scared but also hopeful. The specialist had assured us that this was a very common procedure and we'd have him home with us by that night, or possibly the following day due to his small size. In fact, barring complications, he saw no reason why we wouldn't be able to take him to New York with us.

Dr. B. had done the first catheterization procedure when Joshua was just six days old; he's one of the best in his field, and we liked him and had confidence in him. He read through all the dire warnings with us, had us sign the consent, and warned us of any and all possible side effects of a catheter procedure, up to and including death. We signed the forms and kissed Joshua on the forehead as they wheeled him away to the catheterization lab.

That night was uneventful. Because of his small size, they wanted to keep him for observation, but other than that he looked good. The procedure had gone well and the prognosis was good. This time they felt confident that it would hold. He would be okay, and there should be no need for further interventions. Our hearts were light when we were discharged on Friday afternoon to resume our lives with our three-month-old son.

I had a photo shoot on the Friday night, so Tim drove me down and then he and Joshua went for coffee while I worked. Life really seemed to be resuming its pace, and the catheterization seemed like a small blip in a fairly normal week. All the stress and worry of the past year was over, and now we'd get to enjoy the normal new baby stuff. We went to bed that night confident that our son was well on the road to recovery, and looking forward to our few days away in New York.

The next day, Saturday, April 26, 2008, my mother and grandfather visited. We were on the deck in the back yard enjoying the warmth of spring and our newly planted garden. I was just about to feed Joshua when we noticed a strange rhythmic movement in his arm. It looked like a muscle spasm in his right arm and hand, and it seemed to be in time with his heartbeat. We called the cardiology ward to double check that this wasn't something to worry about. They asked us to go straight to the ER.

By the time we got there, the spasms were affecting his lips, eyes, and right cheek. They were so minor we almost couldn't notice them. The benefit of having a history like Joshua's is that when you get to the ER, they take you in immediately. There's no waiting for hours on end for the first available doctor. The downside is that they keep you a long time, running test after test, because they don't want to be the doctor that missed something.

On that Saturday we waited and waited, and finally I sent Tim home. There were things that needed to get done, and by this time we were convinced that it was just a muscle spasm and he would be released without worry. Tim left, and I settled in for a long wait.

At dinner time when they refused to let me feed Joshua, I became concerned. *What could possibly be going on that he isn't allowed to have food? This is a three-month-old baby, and he's hungry.* He was screaming, and I too began to cry in frustration. They gave me sugar water to put on his soother to ease the hunger, but it only lasted a moment before the tears began again. Tired, frustrated, and scared, I called Tim and asked him to come back. When Tim heard that they weren't letting me feed him, he too began to suspect that something was seriously wrong and came immediately.

At eight o'clock that night, they took Joshua down to the MRI department and put him to sleep with a general anesthetic. They took us to the OR waiting room, where we sat for hours waiting for news. Tim's dad and brother came; our pastor and his wife joined us. We all waited in fear and stunned shock. *This is supposed to be over, isn't it? How are we here again?* It seemed almost surreal, and in many ways, Tim and I were calmer than everyone else. But it was a mighty blow to our already bruised hearts. Our reaction was "Here we go again," while everyone else seemed to be in a panic. Looking back, I believe our calm was a gift from God, yet another star in a very dark night sky.

At eleven o'clock that night, we were finally called into the recovery room to see Joshua. He was still sleeping from the medicine, but even in sleep I could see the little spasms. Being unable to stop them brought a lump to my throat. What was wrong with my son? A doctor came in and took us to the computer with the results of his MRI on the screen. Our son's brain was on a large screen in black and white for us to see, but also to mourn. At some point during the catheterization procedure (they figure immediately after the catheter entered), a blood clot had formed and was pushed up to his heart. Normally it would have gone to his lungs and been forgotten, but instead it travelled through the hole that had never closed in his little heart, the hole they intended to fix when he got big enough. It went through that hole and straight to his brain, causing many little strokes and one massive stroke. Because of the elasticity of his young brain, he has now completely healed, but at that time, the potential damage it had caused was undetermined. They told us that we wouldn't know the full extent until he was older and could have further testing, but the size of that stroke in an adult would be catastrophic.

The news came as a shock. I watched numbly as tears poured down the faces of everyone there with us. It was like watching a movie happen to someone else, and a part of me waited for my own tears, but they didn't come. The brain connection between trauma and emotion and reaction didn't connect. Was God there? Did he know what was happening? Had he stepped out of the room as the catheter was being inserted into Josh's artery that Thursday morning? Some answers I won't receive until I see Jesus face-to-face at the end of my time here on earth. What was the purpose in this kind of injury? It seemed like a cruel joke, or a mistake that the imaging technician had made, rather than a truth that we needed to deal with.

I heard the offers for prayer that night, and I heard the words offered in comfort, but what shook me the most was the panic and fear I heard in their voices. I hardened that night; I felt it and allowed it to happen. I could not allow their panic to get to me. I had to be strong, and to do that I had to be oblivious, even optimistic. This was nothing, a bump in the road. He was alive, and that was all that mattered. I put a wall between myself and the news they shared with me that night, a wall between my heart and the fear that I heard in the voices of our friends and family. It couldn't, wouldn't touch me. I offered up only one prayer, and it was simple: "If you are here, Lord, then allow his brain's plasticity to heal the injured areas."

In those moments after hearing about the stroke, I thought back to Thursday morning when the doctor had gone over the list of possible side effects. Only then did I remember the part about strokes, that one in a hundred chance had happened to Josh. I looked down at his tiny little sleeping body and watched his spasms, now known to be seizures, and asked if we could at least do something to stop them.

The nurse looked at me politely and said that there were no more seizures. I insisted that there were, albeit hard to see. No matter how long she looked at him, she didn't see them, and she began to get annoyed by my insistence that they were happening. I started to seek help elsewhere, and finally another doctor saw the seizures and ordered more medication to stop them. With that taken care of, I had nothing left to do. I stood staring at this tiny little human who had already been through so much, this little life I was responsible for. I could see his chest moving up and down and could find comfort in that. I could see that the seizures had stopped and could watch as rest entered his little body. I held his little fingers, so soft and yet his grip was strong. I could smell the lavender baby lotion that lingered to his sleeper from his morning change. I felt a love wash through me that felt too huge for me to hold—powerful love, protective love, a deep, unconditional love, and I knew that I had no other option but to find a way to figure out what this meant for Joshua, for us.

What frustrated and angered me the most at that time were the reactions of others to the news. When doctors, family, and friends would say that Joshua had brain damage, I could feel the bile rising to my throat. The words sickened me in ways that cannot be described. This was my son, and he would be fine. To label him so young was to damage him for life. It became my mission to ban those words from the vocabulary of anyone involved in my life, in Joshua's life. This was something I could do for him; I could allow him to choose his own path. I had choices in this: I could choose to not allow him to do anything for fear that his health would suffer, or I could choose to allow him to try anything he wanted. I could let him live and in the end trust God and him enough, love him enough, to let him set his own limits. If we had only a week left with him, I wanted that week to be LIVED, not simply lived.

The stroke taught me a lesson of love for Joshua that I hadn't yet realized. I had dreams for him, my own dreams for him, and his stroke threatened those dreams. But they also opened up a door to a new dream, the dream that Joshua could live his life as he really wanted to, a life without limits. He could be free to play sports if he chose; he could climb mountains, travel the world, take on risky adventures, or even just work a desk job or enjoy quiet nights and board games. He could achieve anything he set his mind to, and I wouldn't try to stop him. Regardless of the scary words the neurologist used about brain damage, or what the cardiologists said about his heart, I wanted him to live his life and learn on his own what his limits were, what his passions were, and where his strengths lay. Had they not said only months before that Joshua wouldn't live at all? Now here he was living, growing, and breathing; his heart was beating. What's a bit of brain damage to a God who can do all that? So the words "brain damage" were banished from our vocabulary, and the limits on Joshua became limitless.

When I look back on that stroke and search for meaning in the needless suffering of that injury, I see how God allowed the label the doctors used to free us from the bonds of limits in general, to teach us about making idols of our dreams for our kids or each other. How those stars were shining on those nights, yet I wasn't looking up at the time! I missed them, too busy looking at the ground for my footing. Looking back, I see how my love for Joshua changed, how it became even more unconditional. I see how strongly God loves us. He has removed the limits from us, and he lets us go with open arms. We have the freedom to set our own limits, and he loves us regardless of our choices. I didn't see that love lesson in the moment. I can only share this from a new place of understanding, from a perspective that has come with time and healing.

The next morning, Dr. B. came to see us. Joshua, being the warrior that he is, stuck out his tongue at him. Moments like that made life in SickKids bearable—that and the homemade banana bread that can be found in the cafeteria downstairs, conveniently located beside the coffee machines We were now caught between two departments, cardiology and neurology. The prognosis was to wait and see how things went.

The medications doubled in both amount and expense. One of the vials of medication cost $800 a month. They called it liquid gold, and we had to learn to inject that gold into our son's little thigh twice a day. He was also put on a narcotic to prevent seizures. Add this to all the medications that his heart required, and our lives were soon ruled by drug schedules. With one medication every four hours, one every eight hours, one every twelve hours, and more in between, it seemed that all we did for the first year of Joshua's life was feed him, medicate him, and change diapers. He became so used to the different medications that he would sleep through both the needles and the oral doses.

We settled into a new normal, and thankfully Joshua began to sleep through the night with help from the narcotics. Spring had arrived, and the days and nights were getting longer. We were feeling more able to cope, more willing to deal with what life threw at us. I still wasn't really talking to God. I was talked out, and I wanted to put it all behind us, forget the past year and move forward. I wanted to remain numb, and I also have to admit that I was unsure of my feelings for him or what I wanted to say to him, if anything at all. My pleading hadn't worked, and I was too tired to discuss that with him. I was also thankful, and I knew I was so blessed and loved by him, but the knowing never offered me the true comfort I sought. Perhaps I felt that he'd abandoned me when I needed him most. I was torn between being thankful and grateful but also hurt and angry. I didn't know where to begin in dissecting my feelings.

I didn't want to explore my thoughts or feelings. I stuffed down all of my emotions out of fear that I would have to deal with them, and out of a deep shame that I wasn't being strong enough, or faithful enough. Facing them would mean realizing my deepest fear, that of being a complete and utter failure. Underneath it all was a growing fury at myself, leading to a self-loathing that I couldn't face. I was supposed to believe that God would do the impossible. I'd been asked—no, *commanded*—to be strong and courageous. Instead, I always felt weak with fear and worry. I hid my fear behind optimism and hope and adopted the motto "fake it till you make it." And I did. I even made myself believe it for a time. I called it faith, but looking back now I realize that it was a way to hide. If I could tell myself how faithful I was, then surely God would honour that and do something for my son. I am so thankful that God works for our best regardless of our motives or intentions in times like that.

TEN

ONE NIGHT WHEN TIM WAS AT WORK AND I WAS CHANGING JOSHUA INTO his pajamas after his bath, I noticed an odd, squishy bulge in his groin. I showed it to Tim when he got home, and he thought we should go to the doctor. He thought it looked like a hernia. I had to giggle to myself. *Of course! The kid hasn't had enough crap landing at his door, now he needs a hernia too.* We took him in the following day and, sure enough, the poor kid had a hernia. Apparently, it's quite common in preemie boys. He would need surgery to correct the issue. We were once again talking to doctors at SickKids and now being followed by yet another department.

Around the same time, we found ourselves back in cardiology for what should have been another routine echo and follow-up, but the news was worse than we could have imagined. The catheterization, the same one that had caused the stroke, had not worked. The muscle in the right ventricle had again thickened, causing the space in the right atrium to shrink. The hole that had been created in the cath lab (the one that was supposed to last until he was in his teens) was closing. Since they felt another catheterization held no hope, they decided that open-heart surgery was necessary to repair the damaged valve and close the hole at the same time.

That feeling you get when you're about to vomit, when your skin is clammy and cold and your eyes lose focus? That's how I felt holding Joshua and listening to his cardiologist that day. He was barely six months old, and they wanted to cut him open and stop his heart. They had to be kidding, right? At what point was God going to stop this insanity and do the impossible? All those things that the doctors said were a one-in-a-hundred chance of getting? Joshua got them all, and I began to dread the statistics part of any conversation with his doctors. Surgery was not something we were prepared for, and as I began to grasp its implications, I also began to actually entertain the idea of his death for the first time since hearing about his illness. I feared what that would do to me, Tim, and our families ... but worse, what it might do to my faith.

I sat holding him in the rocking chair in his nursery, the room no one had thought he would ever see, let alone sleep in for almost six months. I rocked him, swishing my fingers over his forehead, and allowed myself to go there, to enter the dark fear that had hovered from the beginning. What if he doesn't make it? What if we're left with only the memories of his short life? How would I walk away from that coffin? How would I say goodbye? How could I place him in the cold, dark earth, experiencing viscerally that he might be cold and scared? How would I breathe under such circumstances? Hour after hour I held him, slowly finding the words to pray again: "Lord, you created this child. This little life is one that you have planned since before time began, and you are fully in charge. I can't say goodbye to him. I don't know how. Please, have mercy on us."

Prayer is funny that way. Long periods of silence go unnoticed, but all it takes is one prayer, one request, one voiced fear, and the rest comes streaming out. I began to pray in earnest again. I explored my disappointment with God regarding his failure to perform a miracle and began to see that Joshua's being here was miracle in itself. And while not the comprehensive one I had hoped for, it was the one I had and was able to cling to.

I sensed God telling me "Don't be afraid; be strong and courageous. I can do the impossible." A flicker of hope came through those dark days. I began to believe again. I began to hear God again. Silence has always been my enemy, and talking to him about my feelings was something I had dearly missed.

The surgery was scheduled for July 21, 2008. They decided to try a number of things in the OR that day. They would try to fix the pulmonary valve, try to close the hole in his heart, and, if possible, try to do the hernia repair. We went through the pre-op appointments and listened carefully with a new ear to all the dreaded "possibilities" that go with open-heart surgery. We held Joshua more and tried to do fun things with him, not for his sake as much as our own. I took photo after photo, recorded videos, and wrote him letters for the years to come. Tim and I talked through all the what-ifs and shared our fears, but again we found ourselves comforting those around us. Pushed for answers we didn't have, we grew tired and emotionally drained long before the surgery date. A cloud loomed before us, but we had no cover from it, and no one was able to offer one.

I had a hard time trying to figure out what was going on in our minds back then, trying to sort out all the feelings in an honest way so that I could properly explain it to you, or even just to understand it myself. A part of me felt very unknown by the people around me; I was new to Toronto and Tim's family and church. His friends were becoming my friends, his family was becoming my family, and the church was becoming my community, but at that time we weren't there yet. Tim and I had been married less than a year at that point, and I had only been back in Canada for two years. I think back and realize that because I wasn't known, I wasn't trusted, and because I wasn't trusted, I had a hard time trusting. It's very difficult to share your real pain when you don't trust.

I was also scared that if I let go and opened the floodgates of my heart, I would break. Every time I had to speak to someone about anything from dinner plans to the surgery ahead, I felt like the tight rope I was on was swaying, just waiting for me to lose my balance and fall. I knew that if I fell, I might shatter into a million tiny pieces, impossible to puzzle back together again. In retrospect, I wish I had done things differently. I wish I'd been braver. I wish I'd spoken up and taken the risk of being known. I see these things now with a clarity that comes from hindsight, and I can see the dark places where my choices led me. Sometimes risking it all to be known is to find a heart that is whole, but sometimes it opens you to deep rejection and sharp criticism. I faced both of them during that time in our lives, and I quickly learned that it was safer to hide

The first time you hide, it's decision that you consciously make. The next time is easier, and before long you don't need to think about it. You wake up and plaster a smile on your face. When asked how you're doing, you say that you're fine, because if everyone around you thinks you're okay, then you can forget for a little while that you aren't. When you're busy forgetting that you're hurting, and that your fear is only being kept at bay by a sheer force of will, you start to lie to yourself ... or at least, that's what I did.

I told myself that I was being strong and faithful. When I saw people around me enjoying the freedom to just say and do what they needed to say and do, I felt resentment creeping in, along with anger and fear—fear that maybe I was already broken beyond repair, that I'd lost something important but was too tired to figure out what that was. Then came the shame that I wasn't strong, brave, or faithful, shame that I was failing as a wife by not being strong enough for my husband. I was a failure as a mother, because my unfriendly womb had somehow broken my son's heart. As a child of God I was failing, because even though I couldn't name it then, I knew deep down that I wasn't handling any of this well but was living a lie, splitting myself into two people and hiding the other woman so deep inside myself that she eventually went silent.

On the day of the surgery, we met with the surgeon, talked to the anesthesiologist, cuddled Joshua, and held his hand while the IVs were inserted, and then we walked the final steps with him to the OR staging area. My lungs hurt from the deep desire to cry; my eyes burned, and my throat ached. Tears threatened to overflow, but I couldn't give in to them. I wanted him to see me smiling at him; I didn't want him knowing a moment's fear. I wanted him to know it would be okay.

The nurse eventually came, took him out of my arms, and walked through the doors to the OR and out of sight. My arms felt as empty as the day they'd taken him from me six months before. The room was full of families. Nurses, orderlies, and doctors were bustling about, getting ready for surgeries. The air smelled sterile, yet it all vanished when that door closed behind the nurse. I turned to Tim and let the tears come in waves, as if we were the only ones in the room. It was done. There was nothing more we could do; we had given control to someone else. So many times I've heard parents say that having a child is like having your heart walking around outside your body. That was the day I understood what they meant. God would be his only source of comfort now, and he and the doctors were all I had left to hope in. We found seats with our families in the waiting room and began the intolerable wait.

Shortly after the surgery started, we looked up to see the surgeon standing before us, beckoning us to a private room. My stomach dropped and I felt the panic rise. This couldn't be it? That couldn't have been the last time I held my baby, right? Your mind and heart go the entire gamut of feelings and thoughts, and they're not easy to revisit. It still holds the power to choke me up to relive that moment. But the doctor only wanted to let us know that he would not be attempting the hernia repair. The relief was so real, so full, that it got me through the next few hours without too many other feelings. We sat there, trying to read, trying to eat, drinking lots of coffee, until the doctor returned about five hours later.

The surgery had been semi-successful. Cutting the hole where the pulmonary valve should be and leaving it open wasn't a permanent solution, but they estimated that by the time Joshua needed the valve replaced, he would be in his late teens or early twenties. With the rapid rate of medical research, it was possible that there would be no need for open-heart surgery. At this point in time, the hole between the chambers couldn't be closed because he was too little, so they'd cut the flap to help minimize the fluctuation in his saturation levels and create a more even flow.

The next few days, however, were a roller coaster that seemed to have no end, with no one at the wheel. Joshua's saturation levels got worse.

He was heavily sedated, and to the casual observer he appeared dead. We were told that things would get worse before they got better, and while we tried to prepare for that inevitability, nothing really prepares you for it. No one can tell you what to expect or to feel, not even those who have travelled the road before you. With your own child, it's always a separate and painfully lonely journey. To walk into the CCCU and see your baby for the first time after open-heart surgery—to see his scar, the intubation tubes, the direct lines, the pacemaker wires, the chest tubes—is one of the scariest things you could ever experience.

On the night things were really bad, Tim had to run our small home group, so I stayed at SickKids and found myself in the empty chapel on the hospital's first floor. I yearned for comfort, I so longed for God's touch, his words, his promises, I would have taken anything he was willing to give me. I prayed, I cried, and I pleaded, but nothing came— no words, no comfort. I was met by silence. I sat alone on that cold, wooden bench and wept with despair.

I heard the chapel's back door open but was scared to look, convinced God himself was coming to talk straight with me. The footsteps went in the other direction; the person who entered sat in the pews to the side of me and said nothing. I heard their silence. They heard my tears, and I felt more alone than ever before. But then that person came over and gently touched my shoulder and sighed "Oh my." Although I never saw that person's face—didn't know if it was a man or a woman—that soft touch and heartfelt sigh brought comfort. I can still close my eyes and feel their touch, hear the sigh, and know that person was sent by God in my hour of need. I went to bed that night and began to talk with God again, sharing with him all my fears, doubts, and odd theology around suffering. I wrote the prayer down because I was simply too tired to think clearly, and I wanted to be clear. I wanted to know that God would not only hear me but fully understand me:

"Father, I feel like I have lost the ability to pray. I have no comfort from you. This just seems to get harder and harder. Since the moment we had that first fetal echo, I have been praying for a miracle of healing for Josh, and you don't seem to want to give it to us. Instead of healing him, he just seems to get worse, culminating in this surgery and now these new complications. I am so confused, Lord, and so tired. He's such a sweet baby, Lord. Please, please, please heal him. Lord, I am praying boldly; turn this around for him, for us. You are the only one who can heal him now; I am begging you to do that for us. I trust you, that you have a plan for Josh, and Tim and I know that there is, hidden somewhere in here, a purpose, even if we don't see it now. Father, if I am honest, I have to say I don't understand. I find my faith lagging, and I am scared that it's my faulty faith that is the reason Joshua hasn't had his miracle yet. Please, show me, talk to me, don't be silent in this. I need you more now than I have ever needed you before. I need so badly to feel like we aren't alone in this, to know that you are sitting in the CCCU waiting room with me, that you are near his side, offering the comfort that I can't.

"I am so tired, Lord, and I can't concentrate on you. I can't pray without falling asleep. I can't hear you, Father. I need you to YELL, scream, and do whatever you need to do in order to get my attention. Please, Lord, tell me something, talk to me, and heal my son. Lord, help Joshua.

"You have always answered me when I have prayed. You have never let me down; please answer me now! Don't leave me here alone in this place tonight, Lord. Sit with me, hold me, comfort me. This place is dark and scary, and I don't want to be alone. Answer me, Lord. Hear my prayer and have mercy on me!

"There are so many concerns with Josh, Lord. Heal his bone, ease the pain that it causes him, fix his valves, close the ASD. Lord, I beg you to lift his SATS so that a new surgery isn't needed. You are my only hope. The doctors are about to give up on him. Please, God, please step in now and do something. I own your promise that nothing is impossible for you. This is not impossible; you can fix this. Please, Lord, please fix it.

"I am sorry, Lord. I am sorry for the anger I am feeling, for the hopelessness and the lack of faith. I am sorry for the doubts and for the selfishness. Most of all, Lord, I am sorry for trying to go through this without turning to you sooner. Forgive me for the ways I have failed you. I am so sorry. Help me to believe. Give me faith, Lord, where mine has failed me, and Lord, I pray that you grant us peace, regardless of the outcome. I know we will need your peace.

"Help me to be the mother I need to be, the mother you created me to be, the mother that you entrusted with the care of Joshua. If you take him, Lord, if this was only a temporary stop for Josh, then I ask you to help me to be strong enough, to find the strength of character, the gift of hope and peace, and help me to find a way to continue. Lord, help Tim and me find a way to move through it together. Father, in all this chaos, help us to see your face and feel your arms. I miss your voice; I miss your strength and comfort. I miss your guiding hand."

ELEVEN

ON THURSDAY MORNING, DESPITE NOT BEING OFF THE OXYGEN YET AND not doing very well, Joshua was moved from the CCCU to the step-down unit on 4D. Tim and I were thrilled, because it meant things were looking good. We heaved a collective sigh of relief, and the nurses and Tim convinced me that I should go home, shower, and get some rest. We slept well that night, my heart lighter for the burdens I had left at the cross the night before, and the knowledge that God was indeed looking after our son. I suppose that's what made Friday morning that much harder.

We arrived at the hospital with smiles on our faces, rested and ready to face the new day. We walked into the step-down unit and heard a symphony of alarms and whistles. Nurses and doctors surrounded Joshua's bed, and when I saw the monitor that showed his saturation levels, they were so low that I made a joke about it, asking if the machine was broken. Our cardiologist, Dr. R., who under normal circumstances was very light-hearted and fun, turned to me with worry in her eyes and said, "I'm afraid not."

I stood there helpless while they worked on Joshua. Tim and I held hands so tightly that I can't imagine we had any feeling left in our fingers. Questions flooded my mind, but I was scared that I might distract anyone if I asked them. What had happened? I'd been at home sleeping, resting light and easy, while my son lay here struggling to live? What kind of mother does that make me? God, where are you? You were supposed to be here. Why aren't you helping him? Paralyzing fear filled me as I watched my son turn an unnatural bluish-grey color. His core was the only part of his body with any shades of pink.

After about twenty minutes, they stabilized him, and Dr. R. had the nurses put Joshua into my arms to keep him calm. I held him and fought the desire to run with him from this place, from this fear, from what was happening. You know the expression "your blood runs cold"? Well, it really does do that. When fear grips you like that, it puts every sense on high alert, and I was so scared that this might be it. The tears fell no matter how hard I tried to fight them. In that moment, feeling his skin next to mine, his breath and tears mixing and brushing on my arms, I didn't honestly believe I would be able to let him go, not literally or figuratively.

Dr. R. bent down beside me and explained that during the first surgery, the doctor had cut off a flap that was on the hole between the chambers. He had hoped it would even out the pressure and blood flow, but instead, it had caused the hole to become too large; therefore, his blood wasn't getting enough oxygen. I saw tears in her eyes as she said, "I'm sorry, but we need to go back to OR. It's a risky surgery, but I don't know what else to do for him."

In my heart and in her eyes, I knew what she was saying. He wouldn't survive a second surgery in his weakened condition, but they had no other options. Her tears and her apology weren't over the need of another surgery but for our loss. She left us then in order to gather the team of doctors from CCCU and begin prepping him for an emergency surgery. They asked us to leave the room, and we began to make the hard but necessary calls to our families. I spoke to my mom, and from the sound of her voice I knew that she knew this was it. There was no way he'd make it this time. It was over. She and my dad got in the car that day not to come and visit Joshua but to comfort their daughter over the loss of her child. It all seemed so incredibly hopeless, so final, like his fate had been sealed.

The doctors came and retrieved him, bringing him back down to the CCCU in order to prep him. One of the doctors came out to talk with us and said that he had to sedate him to get the tubes in because he was fighting so hard. This child, the baby who everyone was about to write off, was fighting so hard that he had actually pulled out his direct line. It gave me the courage and the hope to pray even harder, to once again boldly ask for that miracle I had been losing hope in. This was an impossible situation, was it not? So couldn't I ask him to do the impossible? I could control nothing but the choice in that moment to do as commanded, to be strong and courageous and put my faith in his promises to me. And so I believed. We were told that they would be taking him to the OR as soon as they could, but hours passed and we heard nothing. Finally, at four o'clock that afternoon, the CCCU doctor came to us in the waiting room with words of hope.

"We don't want to take him into surgery. We've been in meetings discussing his case and have agreed that we want to keep him sedated and on life support over the weekend to keep his saturation levels stable. We want to think it over, make sure it's our only option."

We had time, and we needed to use it wisely. People around the world were notified and began to pray—family, friends, strangers, all one voice calling out to God with one name on their lips: Joshua. It was the longest weekend of my life. We sat on a precipice, and it would only take one blow in the wrong direction for us to fall over. I stood hour after hour by Josh's crib, staring down at his lifeless body, all blue save for his torso. Holding onto his cold, blue fingers, I didn't stop praying. I didn't stop fighting on his behalf.

We nearly lost him a few times that weekend, at one point due to a nurse's error when she went against my wishes and gave him a medication that had been causing him to crash for an inexplicable reason. Doctors had mentioned it in rounds, but the orders hadn't reached the nurse. Even though I asked her to wait until I could speak to a doctor, she gave it to him anyway, believing I was wrong, or that I misunderstood, or possibly was misinformed. I'd only left the room for a few minutes to speak to Tim on the phone, and when I came back, I learned that she'd given it to him. I was shaking with anger and frustration. I stood my ground and told her to go and get a doctor because within minutes Joshua would crash, and the doctor should be there.

Thankfully, probably to get me off her back, she got the doctor. Sure enough, within moments of him entering the room, Joshua started to decline dramatically. They stabilized him, but I was too scared to leave his bedside that night. I was angry; I could literally feel my blood jumping through my veins. The adrenaline fed me the energy I needed. That anger was easy to direct. The nurse hadn't listened to me, and as a result I'd nearly lost Joshua. Through that experience, I discovered that I'd never learned how to appropriately handle my angry feelings. I was a people-pleaser, a peacemaker, and I hated confrontation. As a result, I'd always stuffed the feelings until I'd blow up. As this journey progressed, I would need to find some way to balance it, but I hadn't learned that yet. That night, I sat silently fuming, but I was polite and appeared calm to the nurses and doctors that I came into contact with. No one knew that inside I was on the edge, that at any moment I was afraid I would lose it completely.

Tim and I found ourselves back again in the SickKids chapel the Sunday night of that awful weekend. We talked, cried, and held on to each other. Tim looked up at a piece of art on the wall, of a master with his sheep, and said, "Joshua isn't ours to hold; he's been given to us on loan, to tend and care for, to raise, but he's not ours. We have no ownership of him. We need to give him back to God; we need to let go."

Oh how those words struck me to the core, how they hurt, yet I knew he was right. Joshua was my son, but he was not *mine*. He was indeed on loan to us. This gift was simply that—a gift, for whatever time we had with him. If we tried to hold on to him, we would ultimately smother him and ourselves. We had to let go and trust God to do his mighty work. We sat and held hands that night and prayed for our son, and then we let go together of the control we so desperately wanted to hang on to. We dedicated our son that night to God's keeping. We gave him back in the only way we knew how and then we prayed for the strength to survive the outcome of that decision.

Monday morning loomed before us—all of my hopes, prayers, and desires for a miracle came down to this day. Nothing before or since has mattered more than the meeting that the doctors were going to have that morning.

I mentioned that at the twenty-week ultrasound, when we discovered we were having a boy, we named him Joshua. Looking back, we both feel that God named him. Joshua means "God saves." That morning, through a consensus of doctors and experts, it was decided to attempt a test procedure in the catheterization lab with a new device called an occluder. They would implant the device in the hole and allow tissue to grow over it, hopefully closing the hole completely. It was a test, so when they got into it they could have trouble and discover a need for surgery, but it was the only hope Joshua had. We signed the consent and began to pray earnestly for God's miracle.

Just one hour later the doctor doing the procedure came to see us and told us that the test had gone well. The hole, for the moment, was closed, and his saturation levels were holding steady. He smiled and told us we could go in and see him if we liked. What we saw that day was what can only be described as a miracle. God had heard the prayers of so many that weekend, all calling on his mercy and healing for Joshua, and he had answered. For the first time in his life, Joshua had pink skin. His cheeks were red and healthy looking; his arms and legs, which had spent the weekend cold, blue, and lifeless, were now limbs with oxygen-rich, red blood flowing through them. Our son, given to God, had been returned to us. We rejoiced that day and continue to rejoice every day we have him.

I was reminded of that time when we were hitchhiking back from Budapest in the van with the Greek men, one pawing at my hair and the others talking and laughing in Greek so that we couldn't understand. I remembered fearing that they would do something to us. I had heard so many stories of women killed when hitchhiking, and as I sat squished between two of them, with fear clawing its way up my back, I called out to God and asked him to help. Before I could finish the prayer, the van started slowing down, steam rising from its hood. We pulled over at a rest stop, and my friend and I got out safely with our bags. God had heard my cry for help and had answered. This God that I serve always answers us, of that I have never doubted. The question quickly becomes: Will it be a yes or a no? I thank God every day for a yes that Monday morning; I will thank him for the rest of my life.

TWELVE

WE TOOK JOSHUA TO THE DRIVING RANGE THE DAY AFTER HIS DISCHARGE from hospital. We stood there enjoying the feel of the club as we hit the balls as hard as we could. Joshua lay on a blanket behind us, enjoying the grass on his back and the breeze on his face, and giggling at a butterfly above him.

The rest of the summer was spent recovering, making sure we held Joshua correctly, dealing with the new issue of nightmares, starting up his weekly therapies, including occupational and physiotherapy, and attending endless meetings with different doctors regarding his heart, his stroke, and his impending hernia repair. We managed to enjoy our days and nights together, going to the cottage, playing in the water and sand, swinging on the swings, and napping together in the afternoon sun. My life revolved around making sure this little guy knew he was loved. I wanted to erase any bad memories he might have, and to erase the nightmares as well.

Occupational and physiotherapy took over my life that summer, not just the appointments, but also the daily regime of exercises we were given. I'm not one for routine, so this was difficult for me. The occupational therapist was tough, and her dire predictions for Josh's outcome filled our appointments. She was convinced he would eat like an animal because he hadn't mastered the spoon by eight months. He also couldn't sit up alone, refused to be on all fours, and made no progress with crawling. He was behind in every infant milestone, and every week I heard a repeated litany on how poorly he was doing and how I needed to work harder, push him harder, make him better.

What I heard was what a bad mother I was. Occasionally they would toss me a crumb by saying something like "Every kid develops at different rates," but for the most part, I took it as a failing grade as a mom. What they couldn't know was what I saw every day—he tried very hard, we both did, but we were both so worn out. Rather than give myself permission to take a break, I took it as confirmation of my failure.

In September, we met once again with the neurology department for a routine assessment. I was concerned about his eye contact. He no longer seemed to look at us; instead, he glanced over one shoulder, as if he were unable to see. It looked like his eyes were crossed. The team of doctors looked at him and decided to refer us to an eye specialist. They said it could be a result of the stroke, or it could just be that his eyes appeared crossed because of the extra folds of skin around the eyes—apparently a common thing. So that became another medical department to add to our growing list for Joshua's care, and yet another appointment to add to an already cramped schedule.

SickKids was quickly becoming our second home, and with no room for a social life, I had become quite isolated. I felt like a burden if I spoke to anyone about my real feelings, and in many ways I felt so different from my friends. I'd been changed by the experiences and no longer felt like we had anything in common. Only Tim really understood how I felt, so we clung to each other. It's only now, after Joshua's gradual healing and my own emotional journey, that I realize what was going on at the time. I had become completely numb to what was going on inside of me, which was why one morning while brushing my teeth, I looked into the mirror and didn't recognize the woman staring back at me. This journey of motherhood was not what I had expected; it wasn't the one I would have chosen, but it was the one I'd been given, and I was living in a strange paradox of thanksgiving and dread, fear and joy, hope and despair.

In October of 2008, Tim went on paternity leave. We were given some much needed time to rest, and Tim's parents arranged for a family holiday in Europe. We were to meet them in Rome for a two-week Mediterranean cruise, but we would also travel ourselves through Tuscany, Austria, France, and the UK. Taking Joshua was exciting, mostly because just a few short months before, we weren't sure he would survive. On that cruise, Joshua managed the all- fours position. He was nine months old. By the end of the cruise, he was sitting up on his own. Yes, he was developmentally a little behind, but clearly the kid had strength, fight, and charisma.

The entire ship fell in love with him. At the beginning when they saw us coming, you could read their expressions: "Uh oh, baby on board," just primed to cry and drive them crazy and disrupt the quiet, peaceful cruise. But by the end of the first day, people were coming up to us to comment on how good and sweet he was. He was either happy and cute or sleeping and cute, and other than one or two fusses for the entire two weeks, he was an angel. He was so loved by the other guests that people who'd never met us knew him by name. At the end of the cruise, Tim and I were strolling around Venice when a group of six older couples came up and said, "Oh, it's Joshua! Can we take a picture with him?"

It was also on this cruise that I felt the weight of emotions I had ignored for so long. Anger, fear, sadness, worry, and doubt bubbled over. I have since read studies that conclude that parents going through trauma with a child are often so overwhelmed during treatment, they're unable to focus on themselves while taking on the bulk of the emotional impact for the family.

I read a lot of books and articles by pediatric psychologists who refer to the parents of critically ill children as being in a war, fighting on the frontlines. As we know from war veterans, no soldier comes home unchanged, and some suffer terribly with anxiety, depression, and PTSD. I knew none of this while on that cruise, and I couldn't have articulated what I actually felt, except that my buried feelings were emerging as anger. The smallest slight, perceived or real, would set me off, because a word could re-open a wound that hadn't yet healed. It was like balancing a bucket of water, and adding another drop would cause the bucket to tip and spill its contents on anyone in its wake. It was getting harder and harder to keep it balanced.

At times I was chastised for allowing this anger out, and for sure there were times when I over-reacted, but it confirmed what I had always believed—my emotions are too much for people. They didn't want to know me, the deep-in-my-heart me. The mask I wear, the easy going one, is far more likeable. I've been given this message many times in my life. My feelings always come with tears, even a commercial can cause my eyes to leak, and too many times I had been told not to do that, that it was either a tool of manipulation or weakness. I always felt it was more comfortable for people if I didn't "emote" in that way. They liked it better, liked me more, and at the heart of it all, I'm a people-pleaser who hates conflict and wants people to like me. So I appease them and hide and stifle until that ticking bomb goes off, and heaven help those on ground zero. I know it was fear that drove me, the fear of being rejected, but I also lived with the fear of that bomb inside of me. I was afraid of doing or saying something I'd regret. I could hear and feel the ticking, and I seemed to know that I had no control over it. I wasn't even sure who I was angry with, or what I was angry about, aside from Joshua's unceasing fight for survival.

It also didn't help that *everyone* had an opinion. One time, an American tourist standing at the Pantheon in Athens saw Joshua's cheeks chapped from teething drool and actually pointed her finger in my face and told me, "That child has wind burn; he should be inside." Everyone seemed to know how best to raise Joshua and wasted no time pointing out what they thought was wrong.

On the flight from Venice to London, we sat beside a man who quietly watched Joshua before asking if we were his parents. He then stated the obvious: "His eyes are crossed. You should get that fixed." On the flight from London to Toronto, after having been in transit for eighteen hours between the Paris airport and the London tube, with a stroller in rush hour, Joshua, exhausted and thrown off by a change in his nap schedule, began to cry, which soon turned to screaming. I moved to the galley with him so that I could hold him and try to get him to sleep, but he was fighting sleep hard. A woman standing in line for the washroom turned a few times and glared at me, clearly annoyed by the crying infant. Then, in a voice loud enough for me to hear, she said to the woman in front of her, "That child does not want to sleep; she shouldn't force him."

I realize it probably would have been wise to ignore it, but instead I told her in words that were pleasant but a tone that made my actual feelings very clear that she should mind her own business. I knew I had let some of the lava erupt. I felt my blood pressure rise and my cheeks heat, and I knew that my reaction was being frowned upon. I had been judged and found lacking. I kicked myself the rest of the flight home for allowing my emotions to be seen, and in the process, I allowed more lies, guilt, resentment, and shame to take root in my heart. I see now that it wasn't my emotions or feelings that were the offensive but rather it was my inability to control or manage them. Hindsight, as they say, is 20/20.

My anger with God was my biggest struggle. He had saved my son, so how could I still be angry? Was I angry? Or was I angry at others? Doctors? Nurses? Family or friends? Maybe it was deeper. Was I really just deeply angry with myself because I couldn't fix this, that I wasn't handling it all better, that I sucked at this whole motherhood thing, that I just sucked in general as a person for the way I wasn't able to do anything right? The anger spilled out on everyone else, including Tim. I would get annoyed for no reason, or for a reason totally blown out of proportion.

I also couldn't sleep without nightmares, and any glance backwards caused a deep sadness. I would lie awake, scared to sleep and afraid of the nightmares, but then I'd get lost in thoughts about what had happened. The sadness would be too much and my imagination would take me down the road to the future, and the anxiety would take my breath away. I was tired, yes, but it was so much more than that.

As we travelled through the Alps of Italy and Austria, the mountain landscape worked its magic on me, and I started to feel again. No longer numb, my heart began to soften, but that only served to expose wounds

I'd kept hidden. The smallest thing brought about great sadness, and I struggled with finding ways to cope. There I was, driving through the mountains that had once inspired my deep love for God, sitting beside my best friend and husband, our son alive and sleeping quietly in the back seat, but I still felt as though I was walking through sludge. Everything took so much energy, and my brain was so foggy and tired, full enjoyment of the moments was impossible.

I assumed that no one wanted to deal with my emotions, a view that also caused me to hide my real feelings. I was the pastor's wife, so I needed to wake up, place a cheerful smile on my face, and be strong and faithful for others to see. But people are people, and sometimes they say insensitive, hurtful things, not realizing that their words hurt deeply. When Tim and I were first married, if he noticed I was upset by something, he'd generate a conversation to draw me out, prompting me with statements like, "I didn't help you clean up after dinner; you should be annoyed with me." He'd then ask probing questions until I finally admitted that, yes, I was annoyed. We joke about this now, mostly because we've learned how to do conflict well over the years, but it's still not comfortable for me, a classic conflict avoider.

Like all conflict avoiders, I would stuff things down until they erupted in inappropriate ways. On my walk to healing, I've discovered that my identity as the strong one who could cope with anything had become an idol of sorts, a way of feeling better about myself. I focused on perpetuating this attitude throughout those first months of motherhood by insisting on keeping peace with any and all. Somewhere along the way I had tried to be my own source of strength, tried to do as God commanded of me. I had forgotten that He is my strength, and, frankly, I had run out of my own.

The night we arrived home after weeks away, I cried until morning, ashamed of the anger, my inability to cope, my lack of joy in life, and my frustration that no one seemed to understand or offer me some grace. But I didn't know how to deal with it. Tim and I talked all night, sharing our thoughts and feelings, thankful for each other.

The road to recovery and healing has been a long and ongoing one, which started with me telling God how disappointed I was in him, because he could have done things differently. I told him how I had wanted the whole "baby thing" to unfold, and how I felt like he had abandoned me when I'd needed him most. I almost felt like he had done the bare minimum to keep Joshua alive, but I knew he was bigger than that, more powerful, more in control, and I felt let down. I dumped it all on God. I thought God loved me, but through this journey I came to question it. No matter how much I read my Bible and begged God to speak to me, he remained silent. I have since come to realize that it was God's way of pushing me to seek him, trust him, and really *know* him.

In November we went to see the SickKids ophthalmologist that the neurologist had referred us to. After a six-hour wait, the doctor finally saw us. She asked me to go through Joshua's stroke history. (What's there to tell, really? He had a stroke. That's his stroke history.) I walked through it with her, and she conducted several eye tests. She decided that his vision was fine; however, there was a wandering in both eyes that would require surgery. It was decided that the eye clinic would co-ordinate with general surgery and they would do the eye repair and hernia repair in one surgery to avoid more general anesthetic than necessary.

Leaving the clinic that day, knowing we faced another surgery, was nothing more than deflating; I wasn't devastated, overwrought, or emotional. "It is what is" is something that Tim and I tend to say a fair amount, even now, years later. I was moving into a place of grumpy acceptance and expectation of the worst yet always hoping for the best.

Joshua was growing so quickly. He was finally sitting on his own without falling over at nearly eleven months of age, and he was such a happy baby—smiley and full of life, only crying if something was wrong, going to sleep at 7:00 p.m. and waking up between 7:00 and 8:00 a.m., and napping morning and afternoon.

THIRTEEN

WHEN I WAS LITTLE, WE HAD A BACKYARD SWING SET WITH TWO SWINGS. My sister and I would spend hours either swinging or spinning on the swing seats until the chains got tight. Then we'd release them to spin the other way faster and faster, making us dizzy. One time, I came off the swing so dizzy, I tripped and fell, scraping my knee. My mom came out almost immediately, scooped me up, and kissed the hurt.

When I watched Josh, so small and fragile, it made me think of how my mother taught me to protect and then to let go. My days were spent holding him close so that he'd never doubt that he was loved and protected, and so that when the times came that I had to let him go, he wouldn't doubt my love and willingness to scoop him up to kiss the hurts if he fell. In many ways, those months were about me trying to bond with him the way I couldn't when he was born.

On January 31, 2009, we celebrated Joshua's first birthday. Our living room was full of friends and family, with everyone, including Joshua, enjoying the cake. Later, when only family remained, we toasted his life with champagne, thankful for this little boy who wasn't supposed to live past birth.

That night I went quietly to God in prayer: "Thank you, Lord, for all that you have done and for all that you will do in Josh's life. I'm so sorry that I have failed you in so many ways; be patient with me, Lord. Help me to feel normal again; help me to let go of this anger, the hurts, the fear, and the worry. Help me to live in the freedom and knowledge of you and our relationship and have that be all that really matters."

On February 22, 2009, Tim and I learned that we were having a second child. We were both thrilled but also a little overwhelmed! A second baby, along with a one-year-old and all the unknowns we faced with him, could get challenging. We felt the same joys as the first time, but with them came fear. Once you have a child with CHD (congenital heart defects), the chances of your second child having the same issues increase from 1 per cent to 5 per cent. While 5 per cent isn't too high, our experiences had taught us to pay close attention to those numbers.

I would lie in bed at night, hand on my tummy, and beg God to spare this one. My relationship with God had changed over the course of Joshua's first year of life; it had been strained in many ways, but it had grown stronger in other ways. I had a renewed faith in miracles, in God, and in his ultimate power and sovereignty, but I no longer had complete trust in his love. I doubted that he loved me enough. I was hurting and had wanted so badly for him to come and speak to me the way he had in Austria, but I always seemed to be met by silence. Somewhere along way I'd become okay with that, deciding that I would rather have Joshua and not feel the love of God in my life. I believed in God and in his power to move mountains, but when I looked at the pain and suffering in the world, I reasoned that he had done enough, and he was busy. We were blessed that he'd saved Joshua, and I was grateful, but I felt alone.

By Easter of 2009, Joshua had his hernia repair surgery, and the ophthalmologist decided that it was okay to go ahead and straighten his eyes at the same time. We found ourselves back in the OR staging area, holding Joshua and trying to keep him from being afraid. For the first time, I wasn't afraid. This was just another surgery, another blip in our weekly schedule. I sat and watched other parents, those dealing with the anxiety of major surgeries and those facing fairly benign surgeries. I was enough of a regular at SickKids that I knew which ones were serious and which were benign, and I envied the benign ones, because it meant they had a healthy child—not that it made their anxiety any less real, but they probably didn't fully realize how blessed they were to have a healthy child.

One mother whose fourteen-year-old daughter had died just two hours before she was scheduled for a life-saving heart transplant said to me as she left the hospital to arrange her daughter's funeral: "Love your son. No matter what he does, no matter what happens here, love your son. Don't let him doubt your love, and hug him any chance you can, any chance he will let you." Then she hugged me and, with tears in her eyes, turned to the security guard who was there to escort her out. Watching her leave that day, I knew I was blessed. My child was breathing; I wasn't leaving without him.

Hurts, disappointments, fears, and suffering happen to everyone. No one escapes, and to measure my pain and suffering against someone else's is not only futile, but it also takes something from their experience of suffering and forces them into hiding, in essence doing to them what had been done to me by others as well as myself.

The surgery went well. They fixed the hernia and straightened out his eyes, and after a short time in recovery, he was allowed to come home, where we snuggled on the couch together for the evening. It didn't escape me that night that I was blessed.

FOURTEEN

THAT SPRING WAS WARM AND FILLED WITH THE FRESH, EASY FEELING THAT comes when winter is truly over, the sun warming not just the body but the spirit as well. We began to get outdoors and play in the parks, walk around streets and shops, and spend time hanging out in the back yard. We also had an ultrasound and discovered that we were having another boy, and we were thrilled. We named him Kaleb that very same day.

As spring turned to summer, we found a wonderful rhythm to life. The three of us played together, and we went to the cottage with its cool northern breezes, sandy shore, and quiet country roads to explore. My growing belly soon felt the kicks and hits from Kaleb. Just as with Joshua, I craved those moments. My hand often rested there, held over him in a protective and gentle way. I'd caress him and talk to him, all the time telling him about his family and how much we looked forward to meeting him and getting to know him. That summer was peaceful, restful. When I think back on it, I remember the warmth of the sun on my shoulders and watching Joshua play beside the lake—no cares, no worries, just the warm sand between my swollen toes.

Because of Joshua's medical history, we were offered a fetal echo for Kaleb as a precaution. Although Tim and I felt it would be a mere formality, we agreed to it. Tim had a meeting that day, so my mom came to keep me company and look after Joshua. As I lay on the table, I studied the technician's face for any signs of concern. I prayed through it all, hoping and believing there was nothing to fear. When it was over, they asked me to wait while they asked if the doctor wanted more pictures, which was to be expected. My mom and I made small talk for few minutes, but Joshua was getting hungry, and at twenty-two weeks pregnant, I was always hungry. My mom took Joshua on the hunt for food, as much as to ease his boredom as feed his hunger.

After she left, I saw the doctor coming down the hall, and I felt my stomach knot up a little with tension. He shook my hand, introduced himself, and led me to the counselling room. It was The Room, the one with the round table, a heart model, a box of Kleenex, and no air. The room where the joy of my first pregnancy was stolen. Realizing he'd forgotten his file, he got up and left, leaving me with my over-active imagination and a deep fear that made me want to vomit. I wanted to run. The air in the room felt stale, but I forced myself to stay there, although I stood outside the door of The Room rather than in it. At this point, there was nowhere to run. This baby was already here, and no matter what the doctor told me, it wouldn't just disappear. We'd have to deal with it. There was nothing I could do to change things. No prayers would make it different, so why try to get my pregnant belly running?

I was in Berlin once, travelling with a friend for a month of holidays from our jobs in Austria. We were staying in a friend's university dorm room and had just come back from the Christmas market. I had eaten a crepe from one of the market stalls; it had tasted so delicious until the last few bites. I'd thought I was just full, but the next morning I knew I had food poisoning. I spent the day so sick. That night I phoned my mom, just to hear her voice and her love. There's no one better to call for comfort when you need it than your mom.

When I saw my mother coming down the hall with Joshua and lunch, I ran to her. She held me while offering calming words, rubbing my hair, whispering, wiping tears, and then making me go back to The Room to face the doctor and whatever he had to say.

When he returned, he greeted my mother, made the appropriate "cute" comments about Joshua, then turned to me and said that there may be a hole in my baby's heart, though nothing nearly as serious as Joshua's diagnosis. There was nothing we could do until after birth. I was nodding, understanding the words much more now that I was more knowledgeable on the anatomy of the heart. I asked all the same practical questions that I'd asked that first time I'd sat in The Room, and he assured me that I would be able to have the baby with my midwife and that we could bring him in after birth for an echo to see how things were. He advised me to contact our cardiologist and ask her if she would take Kaleb as her patient as well. Then he stood, told me not to worry, wished me well, and left the room.

My hand moved to rest on my belly, as if to protect Kaleb from what the doctor had said. My mom and I just sat looking at each other, and slowly we began to get our things together in silence, both of us trying to figure out what we should be feeling, and neither of us knowing quite what to say. That night as Tim, my mom, and I sat around the table for dinner, we finally talked about it. We decided that we were going to try to not think about it, or let it worry us. If at all possible, we would try to forget about it until it became necessary to remember again.

In September 2009, Tim had to fly to the UK to do some research for a project he was working on for the church. He was planning to be gone for just over two weeks, and I would be spending that time at the cottage. We joked about Kaleb coming before he got home, but he wasn't due until November, so there were no real worries. Two weeks at the lake sounded like bliss to me. My hormones were nuts, and I always felt way too hot. Sitting on the sand with my feet in the water was exactly what I needed. On September 16, Tim and I and friends went to the U2 show in Toronto, and the next day Tim flew out while Joshua and I drove to the cottage from the airport.

The first few days were spent resting and playing with Joshua. We had a fun weekend shopping and going to the library and the beach. Joshua enjoyed being with his grandparents and great-grandpa. That

Saturday night around one o'clock in the morning, I woke up feeling incredibly dizzy. I felt like I had motion sickness, and I had trouble walking to the washroom. I hated to wake my mom, because she was doing so much already for Joshua and I. We both needed rest, so I got back into bed and hoped the spinning would stop.

By Sunday morning I felt a little better but chose to stay home from church to rest. But the dizziness and headache came back in the afternoon. After lunch we consulted Dr. Google and discerned that I should check my blood pressure, so we went to Wal-Mart and did a blood pressure test. The results were very high—high enough that my mother made me sit and calm down for ten minutes before trying it again, but the second test was no different from the first. Not sure what to do, we decided to call the midwife in the morning and ask her about it.

The next morning after long discussions with the midwives, I returned to Toronto and met them at the hospital to be checked personally (I don't think they trusted Dr. Google or Wal-Mart). The two-hour drive to Toronto with Joshua and my mom wasn't something I wanted to do if they were just going to tell me to rest, but we made the trip anyway. When we got to the hospital, the midwives had me sit in a comfortable chair for a bit before checking the blood pressure. It was still very high. When they left to consult with each other, my mom took Joshua, who was tired and restless, back to our house for a nap.

The midwives returned a while later and sat down in front of me, leaning in such a way that I knew they wanted me to listen carefully. It turned out I had pre-eclampsia, which I have to admit I'd never heard of, so they explained it to me and discussed the symptoms and risks with me.

Pre-Eclampsia refers to hypertension in pregnancy (pregnancy-induced hypertension) because of high amounts of protein in the urine. It refers to the symptoms as opposed to the causes, and there are a variety of different causes for the condition, with elevated blood pressure being the most common sign.

Pre-Eclampsia may develop from twenty weeks gestation. It's considered early onset before thirty-two weeks, which is associated with increased morbidity. Its progresses differently from patient to patient, but most cases are diagnosed pre-term. Pre-Eclampsia may also develop up to six weeks after delivery. The only known cures are Caesarean section or induction of labour (delivery of placenta). It is the most common of the dangerous pregnancy complications and can affect both the mother and the unborn child. It's the most common cause of death for pregnant women.

A lot of thoughts went through my brain, but I wasn't worried. I didn't feel panic or fear. The baby was okay, and I could take care of myself. I only had a few questions that always seemed to come up after talks like this: Can I still have a midwife? Can I breastfeed? Will the baby be all right? The answers were, for the most part, satisfactory. I couldn't have a midwife for my care, but they would be on hand to care for Kaleb once he was born and during the post-partum period. Breastfeeding would be okay, as would the baby, as long as I took care of myself and followed the doctor's orders. The risk was greater to me than to him, and I was okay with that.

I can't say I was looking forward to the weeks ahead. My symptoms were going to get worse as the pregnancy progressed, but it was what it was and there was no changing it. They went through all the scary statistics, problems, risks, and symptoms related to pre-eclampsia and told me that I was being admitted to hospital to get things stabilized. Then they left me alone to sit. I phoned my mother, explained the situation to her, and asked her to try to come and see me once Joshua was in bed and my dad was there. Then I called Tim's dad and asked him to contact Tim.

With the phone calls made, I sat. I was in an empty room, sitting beside a large window looking down into a green residential park. The quiet unsettled me, as it forced me to be alone and think. I'd grown to hate non-busy times, because being alone made room for the girl deep down inside—hidden, locked away, and silenced—to have her whispers heard, and her tears were louder in the quiet. Staring out of that window and trying to distract myself by imagining my two boys one day playing in a park just like the one down there kept my thoughts clear, busy, and peaceful.

Soon my phone rang. I said hello and felt the relief of hearing Tim's voice, as if he were in the next room and not a continent away. He was worried about me and not sure if he should fly home or not. We talked for a while and agreed to wait to see how the night went and to talk to a doctor before he decided what to do. Then, with a promise to call again as soon as he could, we said goodbye.

That night as I lay in bed with no food, no book, and no magazine, I realized that I only had God now, and I turned once again to prayer. In God's perfect timing, our pastor walked in just as I finished my prayer. Tim had emailed him to let him know I was in hospital, and he'd come right away. My mother then showed up with food and drink. I can't remember what the food was, but I remember it tasted so good. I'd been one of those consistently hungry pregnant women. It wasn't long before I was asleep—comforted, loved, and well fed.

The next morning the doctor came in and introduced herself to me. She explained pre-eclampsia and the issues that may arise and told me how they were going to stop any complications. She explained the medicines I would need to take to control my blood pressure. She was concerned about the condition of my kidneys, but she was relaxed and seemed to have it all under control. I liked her; she was calm, nice, and willing to take time to answer my questions.

They took me to the non-stress test room. By this time I knew the drill, so with a book and my phone, I settled in for the twenty minutes of "non-stressing" while trying to block out the monitor's noises. The nurse came and sat me down in a wheelchair to go back to my room. I asked why I couldn't walk, and she patted my shoulder and explained that bed rest meant I took the wheelchair. I was surprised by this, as nobody had mentioned it to me. The thought of weeks in bed made my skin crawl (although I would happily take a solid week of bed rest at this point in my life, on a beach in a cabana, with food and drink delivery). I asked that poor nurse a lot of questions on the trip back to my room, but all she would say was that I needed to keep calm because my blood pressure was high. Keep calm, rest, relax, and take care of you. I think back to that simple message and wonder sometimes if that wasn't the point behind it all. Rest, relax, keep calm, and be still. Take care of you so that you can take care of them. I didn't learn that then, and I still struggle with it now.

I was returned to my room and helped into my bed. Ten minutes later, a new doctor arrived, introduced herself, and examined the non-stress test results. She said they were moving me to the delivery room because contractions were about six minutes apart and the baby wanted to come now. She then whisked me to another room, where I was left on an uncomfortable bed with a thin sheet and no blanket.

I called my mom and told her what was happening. Both of us were shocked. She kept asking, "What? What did they say? Are you sure?" I can giggle now, because it was all so surreal. One nurse was telling me to relax and stay calm, and then a doctor threw me into a wheelchair and rushed me to a room where relaxing is exactly what you're *not* going to do. I waited, and waited, and waited some more. No one came. No nurse, no doctor. I just waited and wondered what the heck was going on. Since I'd never had labour with Joshua, I had no idea what a contraction actually felt like, but I knew enough from seeing other women in labour that something significant should be happening by now, something should be hurting by six minutes apart.

Tim called while I was in that room, and I told him that I was having the baby. He couldn't believe it either. He got off the phone quickly so he could try to make flight changes. I lay there for another hour before someone came in to hook me up to another monitor. Two hours later, they told me that I wasn't in labour, and with happy smiles, they put me back in my wheelchair and took me back to my room. When I was back in my bed, they checked my blood pressure and told me sternly that it was unusually high, and I really needed to try and remain calm. The irony wasn't lost on my roommate and me, and I had a good chuckle when the nurses left. Obviously, some kind of clerical error had taken place, and I felt for the woman who actually was at six minutes apart. I made more phone calls, stopping Tim from altering his plans, and telling my mom not to worry. I wasn't having the baby today.

I spent three days in the hospital; I can't say it was fun. My mom was the only one in Toronto who really knew me or where I was, and she had to look after Joshua. She could only visit once my dad got home from work. I wasn't allowed to wander, since I was on bed rest. If not for my roommate and her husband, I would have been a hot mess of lonely, bored, and non- caffeinated. Finally, my doctor took pity on me and allowed me to go home with conditions. My mom had promised to stay for as long as I needed her, and I promised to stay on bed rest and to return weekly for tests and check-ups. Going home, seeing Joshua, sitting on my own couch, and eating my mom's food was pure bliss. I'm willing to bet that my blood pressure was the best it had been in a week. It was so good to be home.

Meanwhile, I prayed that the baby would stay put until Tim came home. Every day I felt sicker. My head hurt, and almost every night my mother and I discussed whether I should go to the hospital or not. They had said to go in if things changed or got worse, but every day it changed, every day it got worse. Bed rest wasn't hard. All I could manage was Gravol, sleep, and short visits with Joshua. One night, I finally took myself in to the hospital and was seen by a doctor. He told me that I should not take this lightly, because I could die. It became ridiculous, his talk of death alongside his admonishments to keep calm. My mom and I still joke about Dr. Death, which was how I referred to him. I promised to take things seriously and assured him that I'd been trying very hard. After getting my blood pressure back down, he finally agreed to let me go home. He again made me promise to remain on bed rest. The rest of the pregnancy was similar: do I feel "worse enough" to be worried? Should I go in?

When Tim arrived home, I felt so relieved that there'd be someone to come to the hospital with me. With each day getting worse, my doctor decided that we needed to schedule a C-section for Thanksgiving Day, which was Monday, October 12, 2009. A few days before the scheduled C-section, I felt so sick, I had to go back to the hospital. While I lay there waiting to hear the results of tests, my headache changed from bad to really bad, and I started to see blots of light. I was also feeling really sick. Tim got the doctor, and between the two of them they decided that the baby was coming.

The midwives were called, our families were contacted, and the doctor called her husband to cancel dinner plans. The OR was prepped, the sub sandwich I'd been looking forward to was taken from me, and with Tim at my side, looking cute in his scrubs, I was taken on a gurney to prep for surgery. I felt so ill, I was terrified I'd start vomiting while they were cutting me open. I held Tim's hand and focused on taking deep breaths and not throwing up.

Kaleb was born on Friday, October 9, 2009 at 5:50 p.m. He was handed to Tim after he cut the cord and we got to see him, hold him, touch him, and kiss him. It was absolutely beautiful, totally imperfect, but also exactly right. I have a lot of blocks in my memory from that surgery as well; apparently, I repeatedly asked Tim to get me my sub while I was in the recovery. He had to tell me every time that he had eaten it, which made me angry with him. I was also deeply concerned that he pay the parking metre. (We hadn't thought we'd be very long, so we didn't park in the lot.) Tim had to keep telling me that he had already moved the car, which I couldn't understand because I had no memory of him leaving. Then I'd get annoyed with him for leaving me while I was in surgery having his baby. He'd apologize, and I'd ask him to get my sub, and so it went. The man had the patience of a saint.

I made it through the cutting. I got through the baby being taken out, and I even managed to keep it together while they sewed me up. But while the midwives cleaned and weighed Kaleb, I started to vomit. They put Kaleb in my arms, and he and I looked at each other. Then his little lips got hold of my nose and he started sucking, so they put him to my breast, and he started eating like a champ. It felt so perfect, so right. I would hold him, and my body would relax. The vomiting would stop, and the violent shaking would ease. When they took him away, it would start up again.

The pediatrician checked his heart and found nothing to be off. There was no murmur, no signs of any holes or any other issues with his heart. The doctor looked over at me and pronounced him a healthy baby! I felt intense relief and joy, and although there were still health issues for me, I felt at ease knowing that he was okay. My blood pressure took months to regulate, and the toxins that had leaked into my kidneys had done damage. I had trouble with the C-section scar and ultimately was diagnosed with post-partum depression in the weeks following his birth. But he was healthy, growing, and breastfeeding (a lot). When I would sit with Tim and Joshua and Kaleb, I'd feel the completeness of our family. We were four parts of one whole.

FIFTEEN

Kaleb's birth gave us a chance to take our minds off Joshua for a while. We had been given a reprieve from the steady stream of doctor and therapy appointments and could enjoy being a family together. As it was winter, we didn't do much, but we were together—happy, and for the most part, healthy. Tim and I were exhausted to our bones, and we argued at times, but we also shared laughs and good times. Looking back, I see those winter months as a rest, but they were also cloaked in a sadness I was unwilling to address.

In March after Kaleb's six-month shots, he became covered in hives with swelling around his nose. I raced him to Sunnybrook Hospital, listening to his raspy breathing in the back seat. I prayed the entire way. Thankfully, the reaction, though serious and something that would require follow-up, was controlled with Benadryl. I was told to have him tested for allergies before giving him any more shots and sent home with a sleepy but breathing baby. He had a lot of similar reactions, and we couldn't figure out what was causing them. His diaper rash would get so bad, he'd be raw and bleeding, and he was covered in eczema. We used creams and Benadryl to control it all, but no allergist will do tests on a baby that young. So we got used to it and managed with the tips we'd been given.

In May of 20010 we began searching for a home of our own to buy. Around the same time, we had a follow-up cardiology appointment with Joshua. We expected the news to be the same: "There has been no change. I'll see you in a few months for a follow-up appointment and an echo." But we didn't hear those words that day. I sat in Dr. R.'s office, with Joshua in the stroller and Kaleb tucked into my arms, as she rested her arms on the desk and told us that the heart had enlarged beyond what they'd expected. His valves were working too hard, and the ventricle was growing. They wanted to see us in six months to chart the growth, and the doctor talked to us about the likelihood of a second open-heart surgery.

I may have been in denial, but that blindsided us. I still believed that he had already gone through the worst and survived. I had yet to really understand that there is no cure for his illness. I didn't understand that every procedure, every surgery, every new treatment was about buying him time. It took me a long time to comprehend that this was his life; there really was no cure, no magical fix, no medicine that would take away the need for the pain and suffering he would face every time his heart failed. I went home that day in a state of shock. Somehow over the weeks of May and June and throughout the busy summer we managed to put it away, back in the corner of our minds.

In June, Tim took paternity leave and we took holidays with his parents in Quebec City. We also bought a house. In July, we took possession of our home and renovated it from top to bottom. Then we headed out again for a road trip up the US east coast.

Our first destination was Ocean City, NJ, to visit my aunt and my parents. It was my childhood summer spot, and we went to the ice cream parlour, walked the boardwalk, looked in the surf shops, and swam, jumping in waves large enough to engulf us. It was amazing to watch Joshua and Kaleb enjoy the sand and sea and the rides at Playland the way I had as a child. Tim and I took time away from the kids for a night in NYC, where we took in a show, wandered the city, and ate in restaurants in Little Italy. With the break from SickKids, the feeling of the sun still warming my shoulders late into the night, and the smell of salt hanging in the air, it was easy to forget where we had been and where we could be going. We could ignore the dark and ominous cloud on the horizon.

We drove through Massachusetts and Maine, stopping at parks to play and pausing at Boston and Salem and a number of other equally interesting spots. When we got to Maine, we rented a little cottage for a few days. We wandered shops and ate lobster. Tim went fishing, and together we took a four-hour boat cruise to see the whales. It was a bucket list item for me, and I've never been so filled with awe by nature. To see these huge mammals swimming with so much grace and know that human eyes were never meant to view them, that God created all these amazing creatures, from the smallest of the plankton to the largest whales, for his own pleasure is mind-blowing. After Maine we started driving north-west and eventually crossed back into Canada to our new home, all freshly renovated and ready for us to start living our normal lives again.

When Joshua was around two-and-a-half, and Kaleb just a little past one, Joshua finally said "Mommy."

This week Joshua finally is starting to say Mummy for the first time, just this morning he yelled Mummy a bunch of times and then ran up to me, hugging my legs nice and tight. I think back to the moments of terror, worrying and fear that he might not come out of all of this... and I am so thankful, and I find myself sitting here in a place of awe and wonder.

~ Through the Lens of Motherhood ~

Over the course of that summer, Joshua's frequent tantrums that I'd originally passed off as the "terrible twos" got worse, and he was increasingly lethargic and not really gaining much weight. Many things can cause these symptoms, and since it had been a summer full of changes, I minimized their importance. We'd been to our clinic check-up in late May for an echo and ECG. We knew they were charting his heart growth, but I was very good at forgetting or hiding from the truth. I wasn't overly concerned, but I had a nagging feeling about the small symptoms I'd observed.

In late October, we took the boys on an old steam train ride near Uxbridge, Ontario. Joshua was crazy about Thomas the Tank Engine at the time, and trains of any sort were a huge thrill for him. That was the day we realized that Joshua was seriously struggling. Despite his love of trains and the excitement of the day, by the time we got him back in the car, he was so lethargic, Tim and I had to acknowledge what we'd seen all summer; it was time to call his cardiologist.

Around the same time, I gave Kaleb his first peanut butter sandwich. He had barely tasted it when his face started to swell, his eyes growing to three times their normal size. As we raced him to the ER down the street, they continued to swell. His nose and face were unrecognizable, and I regretted not calling 911. Tim drove me right up to the ER bay doors. I hopped out and grabbed Kaleb. I wasn't even through the doors when a paramedic rushed over and said, "That child's in anaphylactic shock; come with me." She raced us through, and the doctor immediately gave him a dose of epinephrine and some Benadryl. It wasn't until the meds had been injected that I noticed the shaking in my hands. The paramedic saw me notice it and gently put her hand on my shoulder and telling me that it would be okay, that he would be okay now. But all I wanted to do was cry. I looked at her kind face and whispered, "This is my healthy child."

I did a mental check through all the household things that contained nuts so they could be thrown out as soon as we got home. This latest development pushed us up the line, and an allergy appointment for Kaleb was made immediately. It was discovered that he had a whole host of allergies, the most serious being peanuts. We would never be without the EpiPen now. Between the two boys, I began to see my life as a series of appointments, anxiety, and potential threats around every corner. Tim and I felt like we were in a constant state of readiness, waiting for the other shoe to drop on us and shift our world again.

Keeping life normal was difficult when there was an obvious decline in Joshua's health, along with the new issue of Kaleb's allergy to nuts.

After more tests, we discovered that he was allergic to eggs as well. One day I took the boys to the gym with me so they could play in the daycare while I worked out. We'd done nothing strenuous all morning. They'd been in the stroller while I ran errands. After lunch we went to the gym, where I explained to the daycare staff about Kaleb's peanut allergy, showed them the EpiPen, and then left them for ninety minutes. Halfway through my workout, the caregiver came and told me that Joshua's face was abnormally red.

I immediately went and placed my hand under Josh's shirt and could feel his heart racing. I told them that while he was probably fine, I would take him home. Why I felt the need to reassure strangers is still anyone's guess. Maybe it was second nature by then, or maybe I was trying to keep myself together. Whatever the reason, I did my best to appear calm while I gathered up the boys, signed them out, and strapped them into the stroller. It wasn't until I was on the street that the panic struck and my hands started shaking. I called Tim and told him that I would get Joshua to ER and drop Kaleb off to him at the office.

Once we got to the ER, they ran tests and took X-rays right away. The results were disheartening. His heart was visibly larger on X-ray, but since our cardiologist was on holiday, we had the choice of seeing another doctor or waiting for our scheduled appointment the following week. I decided to wait, and we went home.

Someone once asked me about how to break down God's love into a really simple understanding ... at the time I felt that was like asking someone to explain quantum physics to a third grader. Until I had children.

The love you have for your kids doesn't seem possible, but you care about every tear, every scrape. When they do something mean, or hurtful, I know I need to teach them a better way, to help them grow into strong, compassionate men.

I can't tell you what God's love is like, but the love I feel for my children is only a fraction of it. Nothing can separate us from that love, not even ourselves.

- Through the Lens of Motherhood-

SIXTEEN

THE FOLLOWING SUNDAY AS I PRAYED IN CHURCH, I HEARD THE PRAYERS for Joshua. I couldn't stop the tears from coming. Hearing his name out loud after all that time brought me back to the beginning, and it physically hurt. I wasn't the only one crying that day as the prayers were said. This kid had stolen a lot of hearts in his short time here. Seeing the tears of others and knowing that they fell out of a love for Joshua and our family brought comfort to me that morning. In that moment, I didn't feel as alone. I felt the weight of the tears on those faces, and it was like my weight was spread out. They were carrying us in prayer, love, and true concern. Still, I kept wondering when it would end. Hearing those prayers made it more real. Joshua was not okay; his heart was visibly larger, and he had had some strange things going on.

People would see him and think he looked great, which he did in many ways. One woman even said, "To think we were all so worried about him." Yes, he looked so strong and healthy, but he wasn't. It was only by a miracle that he was that strong, as most cardiac kids are frail and pale.

As a pastor's wife I placed a lot of unexpected expectations on myself. I thought I had to act a certain way and be an example. I thought I had to be stoic, full of faith, trusting always in God's healing power and love, showing no weaknesses or doubts was the way to go, the way that was expected of me, and the way I expected of myself. I couldn't truthfully tell people how I was doing. I allowed no room for doubts, no room for them to see the cracks. As a result, I built a wall between myself and the very people I needed for support, the community God had placed us in for that very purpose.

The week following our experience in the ER was difficult, as we were also waiting for our next echo. Something was wrong but we didn't know what, or why. Joshua's heart, we were told, would be able to tolerate having no pulmonary valve until he was at least in his mid-teens or early twenties. He was not yet three years old. We watched him closely. Every time his cheeks got too red, we wondered if we should take him to the ER, and I think my hand permanently hovered over his chest that week. I checked his heart constantly, sure it could stop at any moment. The nightmares started up again in full force, in which monsters or bad guys were trying to get my children, and I was unable to prevent them.

Loving and empathetic emails and blog posts kept us going through the scary wait. Our support system had grown, and our community rallied around us despite the wall I had erected. They found ways to love us and show support. Regardless of how many times I said I was fine, I would get a hug, or a freshly-prepared meal would show up at our door. It was like that starry night in Austria. When I looked up, every email, message, hug, or meal was like a star in the dark night, together creating enough light that we could almost make out the next steps.

I began to see that I had perceived God as a puppet, someone to manipulate for my needs. But that god was a false one, a god I had created to manufacture control of the situation. The real one loves me, but he never promised a pain-free life; in fact, he promises that life with him means taking up the cross and following him. Somehow during Joshua's life, I had forgotten that God. I was so consumed by frustration and anger that God hadn't done things my way, the way that brought things under my control and made it easier for Joshua and me. I had allowed myself to become discouraged, believing that it was futile, that God was going to do what God was going to do, and it didn't matter what I did or didn't do.

Not that long before I met Tim, I was willing to suffer for God if it would bring me closer to him. I even boldly dared him to "bring it on," and guess what … he did! And then I ducked and ran. The God I loved and worshipped wanted my complete trust, which, when you think about it, demands every part of me—my heart, mind, and soul. I can't place my son in front of him, nor can I create a false god. I needed to trust God to give me the strength to love him enough to do just that. He was bringing it, and I needed to stop running and start trusting.

He who loves father or mother more than Me is not worthy of Me; and he who loves his son or daughter more than Me is not worthy of Me. And he who does not take his cross and follow after Me is not worthy of Me. (Matthew 10:37–38)

The message was so clear: pick up your cross, lay down your life, lay down your son's life, and follow me wherever I lead you.

SEVENTEEN

On November 3, 2010, we woke Joshua up very early in the morning for the drive to SickKids. He was such a trooper, helping the doctors and technicians when he could and sitting still for the whole hour of the echo.

The doctors confirmed our worst fears. Joshua was in heart failure, and the only option was another open-heart surgery before Christmas. From the moment he was born, we'd lived with the "worst-case scenario." The only odds he had beaten was still being alive. Bile rose in my throat, and sweat coated my palms, but on the outside, I was calm—the tip of the iceberg on a windless day. There was no way to see the hugeness of what I had hidden under the surface. The doctor talked us through next steps and booked appointments for pre-ops. I found myself smiling and saying, "Okay, thank you. See you in a week."

I started taking a power yoga class around that time, trying to physically exhaust myself so I could sleep, trying to sweat the tears out so they wouldn't leak from my eyes. I began to use the cool down part of the class to pray, whispering my feelings to God—not anger so much as questions. Why was this happening to Joshua, to us, again? God put the book of Job into my mind, which starts with a conversation between Satan and God. God grants Satan permission to test Job, whom God trusts, but the testing must stop short of Job dying. It gives us a bird's-eye view of God's perspective. But since Job wasn't privy to the conversation or God's perspective, he had to live out the story blind. He had to endure the suffering without any answers, but somehow he found a way to praise God in the end. Rather than run away or rebel, Job chose to stay and praise God.

I had the same choice—to accept God's everlasting goodness and love and to trust in his promises, to trust that he had Joshua's life and ours in his hands, and to praise and thank him. Or I could continue to run, doubt, and try to control things. I was in a strange place as we navigated the weeks leading up to Joshua's next surgery. I felt closer to God, finding comfort in the community he had placed us in, but still trying to be the strong pastor's wife. But at night, lying in bed, my brain refused to shut down. I began to dread bedtime, unable to escape the memories. I stayed awake until my eyes were sore.

In the morning, I'd find some hope and peace to get through another day, seeing all the blessings that filled my life: Joshua and Kaleb bugging the dog, giggling at bath time, or playing with the trains together. In the daylight we were a normal, young family, and I could see how God was embracing and hearing me. Then the night would come, and it would begin again.

I still seem to focus much of my writing on Joshua and his struggles, but Kaleb was there through all of it. I didn't love him any less. He had struggles of his own, and we dealt with them the best we knew how, but the cloud of congenital heart defects always overshadowed everything. My deepest pain was where my writing often led me. However, there is no one in this world like Kaleb. He is the most loving and compassionate child. Watching him grow and develop during that space of time became an outlet of joy for me. I delighted in him.

At three, Joshua was still not talking, but Kaleb was developing language, constantly gaining new words and asking what things were. I loved the excitement I saw in him as he saw the world through eyes of discovery. I'd get excited to see what came next. Yet he always seemed to be the forgotten child. He was a little gift from God that helped us forget for a while that Joshua was sick. It also helped Joshua forget, as the two of them played together, and I could see the bonds of friendship already being forged.

While waiting for the surgery, we decided to take holiday time to rest up and prepare, staying first with my parents for a week and then having Tim's parents come for a week while Tim and I took some evenings alone. The best laid plans, as they say. Everyone got the flu, and the first week was spent either being sick or taking care of someone who was. The second week, in which Tim and I were supposed to get away together, was also foiled. I was so disappointed and discouraged, so I talked about it with my dad, who later wrote me an encouraging email with one clear message: Be still and know that I am God.

In the insanity I had forgotten to be still; instead, I was spiraling, trying to find answers or cures, even in sleep. Not once did I just rest in God's sovereignty, placing all my fears, hurts, discouragement, and frustration at the foot of the cross. I had forgotten that God was in control, and God is not chaos. He has the beginning and the end all worked out, and he knows Joshua, he knows his doctors, he knows me, and he knows what we all need. And he will see to it. My job as a mom is to love them the best that I know how. I had to stop, rest, be still, and let God handle it.

EIGHTEEN

THE SURGERY DATE WAS SET FOR DECEMBER 6, 2010; JOSHUA WAS NOT yet three years old. We were given the dates for the pre-op and told to go for a dentist pre-op as well to ensure that he'd be safe from infection. We only had a few weeks to prepare him and ourselves for yet another surgery. This time he wasn't a baby who had no idea what was happening to him. This was a child who, though not yet talking, fully understood us. He sat on my lap and listened to the doctor talk about surgery, and he cried. He heard the words "SickKids" and looked at me with frightened eyes. This child knew more than we were giving him credit for, and it became my mission to make this as easy for him as possible. We had him meet the child life specialists, who are better prepared to explain this type of surgery to a child. Everything you can imagine doing to prepare a child for something like this, we did, but I still felt like I wasn't doing enough. I couldn't stop it.

The pre-op appointment was on a Thursday and was scheduled to last the whole day. I had a friend babysitting Kaleb, and another one coming with me to the appointment to keep me company and remove

Joshua from the room if needed. Tim had an important meeting that day and couldn't be there. The surgeons walked through the entire surgery with me and gave me the list of things they hoped to accomplish, as well as all the risks involved.

The first and most important job was to replace the pulmonary valve. They preferred to use a pig valve, but size would be a big issue. Joshua's heart was very small and the space between his chest wall and heart would need to be large enough to tolerate that. The smallest pig valve was still two millimeters too big for the size of his heart, though they thought they could work with it. The secondary option was a bovine valve, but it wasn't the first choice for Joshua.

The second and equally important issue with Joshua's heart was the leak in his tricuspid valve; it was severe and causing many of the problems. They would attempt to fix the leak and get it from severe to mild. If that wasn't possible, they might have to replace it. That was something they repeatedly told me they would not want to do. The risks involved for a guy his size were huge, but the doctors felt there was no other option.

After going through the surgery process with me, they went over all the things that could go wrong, up to and including death. Always the same list, always the same fear. At the very end of the day, a nurse came in to show me how to bathe him the night before surgery and to tell me what to expect. All I could see in my mind's eye was Joshua at six months old— still, lifeless, and blue—dying before our eyes—only alive because a machine gave him the oxygen he needed.

I went home that night exhausted and with a head full of images and words that made no sense to me. Why does this happen to little children? What had Joshua done to deserve this amount of torture? What sin had Tim or I committed? Is this really just the result of a fallen world? I kept waiting for God to reveal how he would turn this story into one for his glory; I kept searching for an answer to the whys. In the end, there were no answers to be had.

I was given choices at the pre-op appointment, but the choices were life-altering. My answers held his life in balance. It seemed to me that the "choices" were just an alternative way of telling me what I had to do, a way of making me feel like I had a little bit of control over the situation. They explained all of the reasons why open-heart for Joshua would be difficult, risky, and very long, and that many things could go wrong in the OR. Some of the decisions couldn't even be made until they were inside his chest. After all of this, they gave me the choice: do the surgery, regardless of risks, or watch him die of heart failure. The statistics for mortality in this particular type of surgery quoted to me that day were one in twenty.

The following morning, we'd be handing over our baby to a team of people in whom we placed our trust for our son's life. Doctors come from all over the world to study at this hospital, to learn so that children in their home country can benefit from the knowledge gained through our research. That didn't change the fear I had handing over my son and signing the consent for them to stop his heart.

I only had one real choice, and that was to trust the God of the universe who had created every living thing up to and including Joshua, the God who had "knit him" in my womb (unfriendly or not). He had a reason for creating him, even if we didn't have all of the answers. He had shown me love, mercy, and grace throughout my life, more than I deserved. He would comfort Joshua in ways that I couldn't. He would be standing beside the surgeons, whispering advice, guiding their hands. Tim and I could live anywhere in the world, yet we lived in Toronto, home to one of the best children's hospitals in the world

NINETEEN

On December 5, my parents came to pick up Kaleb and take him to their place for the duration of Joshua's hospital stay. Though we tried to be upbeat and have a nice visit, none of us really wanted to be there. After my parents left with Kaleb, we made Joshua's favourite dinner of lasagna and sat on the couch to eat it while watching *Toy Story 3*. The suitcase was at the door. When the movie ended, we gave him his pre-surgery bath with a special disinfectant soap. He laughed and giggled while we played. The bath over, we dressed him in new pajamas, and put him to bed. We read a story a friend had made. It was all about Joshua going to the hospital and ultimately coming home. It had pictures of Joshua and the people and toys he loves, and of the hospital, the OR, and the doctors and nurses. It was a story to prepare him but also a story of hope, that this was going to be temporary and he'd be coming home to his family, his big boy bed, his favourite toys, and his dog.

Once Joshua was in bed for the night, I prepared our things for the next few weeks: Joshua's bag of toys, his communication cards, his puzzles, his diapers, wipes, and food for Tim and me to eat that would be better for us than the stuff they serve at crazy prices in the hospital cafeteria. Knowing this would be a night of nightmares and little sleep, we went to bed anyway. By morning, I felt sick to my stomach and had a headache from lack of sleep and too much worry. We got Joshua out of bed, put him in the car, and made our way to the hospital, full of false bravado. It was still dark outside, mirroring our innermost thoughts.

A nurse we'd come to know well greeted us at the hospital. She was a kind, faithful Christian who had cared for Joshua on many occasions. She weighed him, bathed him again, and dressed him in a hospital gown that was miles too big for his small body. She walked through the schedule with us, making sure we had no last-minute questions, and then she turned on the cartoon channel for Joshua and left us to our own devices while we waited.

We didn't talk much. We'd skipped breakfast, because Joshua couldn't eat, and we avoided coffee, because he couldn't drink. We just sat there, lost in thought. The anesthesiologist came in to check on Josh, listened to his lungs, and asked us a few questions. I asked him to use the strawberry smelling anesthetic. He then took out a black Sharpie and signed his initials to Joshua's chest so that the surgeons would know they had the right patient. He left. Joshua stared at the black letters scribbled on his white skin. At 7:30 a.m., Joshua was given meds to relax him so that the separation and OR wouldn't scare him, and we played with the train set there.

We didn't wait long. Our nurse soon came for us. Joshua was getting dozy, so I carried him down to the second floor. The urge to vomit from my fear was strong, but so too was the need to be brave for Joshua. The doctors came out and spoke with us, explaining once again all the risks. They reiterated that it would take about four hours, or five hours with complications. Then they turned and asked Joshua if he would like to go with them. He was so wobbly, I doubt he knew what was going on, so he let go of me and took their hands. As I watched him walk through the swinging doors, I wondered if I would see him again. The urge to swoop him up and run away with him was so strong, I had to physically hold on to my seat.

The waiting room for surgery is a large, square box with couches, chairs, coffee and tea, a few nice volunteers, and a TV screen telling you where your child is. For example, when we got into the waiting room, it said that Joshua was in the OR, and it would stay that way until he was moved to recovery. This brings some comfort, because sometimes the recovery stage is long. I signed in with the volunteer so that she'd know who we were. I gave her our phone number and then we settled into our seats, each with a magazine and a coffee.

I never did open that magazine. I can't even tell you what magazine it was. I just sat there, waiting. Every so often I'd get up and move to the hallway that I knew the doctors would come down in order to find me. I'd watch the doors like a mad woman, or stand in front of the TV screen, waiting for it to tell us that he was in recovery. I had coffee after coffee but was afraid to leave to use the washroom. I struggled against panic, had to fight to control my breathing, and shuddered every time someone at the door moved.

At the four-hour mark, I got very antsy. Any time now they would come and tell us how things had gone. I couldn't tear my eyes from the door, unless it was to look at the screen to see if he was in recovery yet. At five hours, my stomach was really starting to rebel, and the panic was coming more frequently. At six hours, seven hours, eight hours I was beyond feeling sick; I had moved past panic to an open-ended five-word prayer: "God have mercy on him." I couldn't think of anything else to pray. I've never been more terrified in my life, yet still God gave me moments of peace. Like every parent in this situation, I wished to take his place, his pain, and his complications. And I had a hard time getting past the fact that I'd signed consent.

At nine hours I began to seriously panic. All the other parents had long since left for the recovery room. What had happened to Joshua? What could possibly be going on that would take more than double the allotted time? How long could his little heart tolerate being stopped? Had there been some kind of horrific complication? Finally, nine and a half hours after he'd gone into the OR, he was taken to recovery. His surgeon came out and explained that the surgery had been filled with complications, that he had been on and off bypass twice, and though they were unable to fix the tricuspid valve to a level they were pleased with, they had no choice but to close him up.

The pulmonary valve part of the surgery had gone well. They had replaced the valve and actually found that they were able to put in a larger one than they had originally thought (meaning a longer time before any need to replace it). The tricuspid valve's leak only moved from severe to moderate-severe, but with the final "fix" attempt they had to do something that made further repairs impossible. The only choice left after this was a full tricuspid replacement. The doctor was tired, they had fought hard that day, and in some ways, they'd won with huge gains, but in others they were sadly defeated. Tim and I didn't ask many questions that night, only if we could see Joshua. Any questions we had could come later; there would be time.

In my church in Austria, we used to sing a song of simplicity and beauty, just three lines starting with "Don't be afraid." It has stayed with me, and I sang it often during that day and night.

Don't be afraid,
my love is stronger,
my love is stronger than your fear.

The couches in the CCCU waiting room are hard, narrow, and not conducive to sleep. I was dizzy with exhaustion but couldn't leave Joshua's side. As the sedations wore off, he became increasingly agitated, and they had to use wrist restraints. His skin was red; he was thrashing around so hard, they worried he would pull tubes. They sedated him again, but it seemed the more sedation, the greater his agitation. Tears slid down his tiny cheeks, and low moans came from his chest. His eyes were glassy and distant. It dawned on me that he might be having an allergic reaction. I'm allergic to morphine, so maybe he was too. I mentioned it to the night fellow, but he dismissed the idea. I asked if he could give him Benadryl, but he said that it would cause more sedation, and he wanted to avoid that. I was frustrated and felt helpless when I finally went to rest for a little bit. When I came back at two o'clock in the morning, I learned that the agitation had become so great, they'd given him more morphine.

I went to the doctor and told him about my morphine allergy and asked about giving Joshua Benadryl. He ordered it, and Joshua's body soon began to rest, his moaning ceased for a time, and his breathing became regular. The battle over the morphine raged for another two days before finally a nurse on 4D (again, one who knew us well) listened to me after watching Joshua thrashing around for twelve hours and screaming "Mommy" over and over and over again. We went to the doctor and begged for Benadryl and a stop on the morphine, and soon enough, Joshua was resting well.

The next morning, the nurse and I went on a campaign to have morphine erased from his care plan and added to his list of allergies. That morning, Joshua woke up for the first time since surgery. He was shaking horribly from withdrawal, and he was still swollen from the allergic reaction, but his eyes were no longer glassy and he was no longer rolling back and forth, fighting restraints and calling out for me hour after hour. He had a small drink and he even ate a small amount of applesauce.

I don't know what was worse—watching him lying still and sedated in the CCCU, or being more alert and fighting the pain, meds, and irritations that come with surgery. Hearing him call "Mommy" hour after hour reminded me of my totally helpless state, and that I couldn't make this pain go away for him or make the healing process go any faster. But I was thankful that he was fighting, kicking, screaming, and pulling tubes. While painful to watch, it was also a sign of strength. He has a warrior heart, and I thank God every day for giving him a fighting spirit.

I hadn't slept for more than an hour at a time for three days, and I was sick with exhaustion. I would stay the night and Tim would come in around 9:00 a.m. (after shift change) to give me a break. That day I called him at 6:00 a.m. As soon as he arrived, I fell asleep. When I woke up three hours later, Tim was smiling. Joshua wanted to play. With shaky and slow steps, Joshua made his way down the hall to the playroom, where his beloved Thomas the Tank Engine awaited him.

He could barely stand up. His hands shook, his eyes were sunken, and the pain was evident on his face, but when he reached that train set, he looked up at me and smiled. He played a while, and when he got back in his room, he coloured and rested. I tried to get him to drink some juice or eat, but he wanted none of it. That afternoon, our friends arranged for us to have a hotel room at the Delta Chelsea for a few nights so that we could rest and still be close to SickKids. I got there in the afternoon and sank into the bed with its pillows and cozy blankets and fell asleep.

The following night was one of the worst nights with Joshua. He was now angry and unable to sleep because of the pain, but he refused to let me comfort him. He even screamed "No" if I tried to come near him. His post-surgery stomach was bloated and causing discomfort, making it impossible for him to rest. I did everything I could think of, but I finally sat down and cried. I hadn't expected or experienced his anger before, and it scared and hurt me. When the nurse came in, she could see my emotional state and told me to get some air while she took over for a bit. I was gone less than ten minutes before returning to find him asleep, though not peacefully. I lay there for a long time trying to sleep, but his frequent moans had me once again on my knees before God.

When I was first pregnant with Joshua, before we knew about his diagnosis, we went to stay with friends in Waterloo for a night. That night I had a terrible nightmare, one that has literally haunted me ever since. I was deep in the basement of a hospital, alone, and the halls were dark and empty. I was having an ultrasound and I could see the baby in real colour, like the little guy was on TV and not in a black and white, 2D ultrasound. He looked up at me, his big eyes sad and scared. His face was horrific and had a skull-like appearance. I didn't know then that Joshua was a boy, and we hadn't learned about his health problems, but the dream shook me so much I began to pray for him all the time.

That night in the hospital, when Joshua was so angry with me and screaming in his bed for me to go away, I sat on my bed begging God to help us, begging him to give Joshua rest and allow me rest. In that prayer, or in the immediate moment after the prayer, I had an epiphany. There'd been moments during the two weeks prior to his surgery when I had been lying in bed, crying, begging God to help us. One of those times took place when Joshua was screaming in his bed, his heart clearly failing, his body tired, but his mind wanting to get up and play. I prayed that morning for Joshua to know peace, but instead he became louder, more upset, with more tears and screams. The second time occurred while I was in the hospital with Kaleb. The nurse woke him every hour, and Tim and I were beside ourselves with fatigue. I cried out to God that night for rest for us both, for peace, but Kaleb's cries only became louder, and rest never came. That night with Joshua was like the final straw, and I bubbled with anger and frustration. I silently yelled at God, and with angry tears flowing down my cheeks, I vented and spewed about how angry and confused I was. And then the guilt came. *What if God punishes my anger by using Joshua?*

That night, after I'd been yelling at God for not helping Joshua, the nurse came in and gave me a breather. It wasn't the answer I'd asked for, but I had an answer. He had heard my cry; he had entered my frustration and allowed me space to have silence. When I returned, Joshua lay sleeping. God had answered me.

When we'd found out about Joshua's heart defect, my prayers had been "fix it." He didn't do that immediately, and I felt betrayed. When Joshua was a baby in CCCU, I'd begged for help, but it always seemed that whatever I prayed for brought about the opposite effect. Ultimately, my prayers were answered, though not necessarily in the ways I expected or wanted. All parents pray, I believe, even if for those little things when they're at the end of their tether with fatigue or frustration. Prayers like "Please stop this baby from crying," or "Please let me get some sleep." And then there are the big prayers, like "Where are you, Lord, in a country at war, or when children are abused or abandoned?" God asks us to lay our burdens at his feet and leave them there, and He will take care of them and honour them. He didn't say he would do it our way, or on our timeline. But he promised to take care of us. I needed those unanswered little prayers to bring me to a place where I could stop and recognize that I was actually needing to look at the answers I was being given.

The next day, though weak and clearly in pain, Joshua was in visibly better spirits. He would sip on his drink but still refused to eat much.

Tim made his way over to the hotel after dinner, and I settled in with Joshua for the night shift. We watched movies until three o'clock in the morning—*Toy Story 1*, *2* and *3* over and over again. Joshua's anger with me was gone and was replaced by a smile when he would look over at me during a funny part of a movie.

The outpouring of love, prayers, generosity, and support over those days was overwhelming, and as a family we saw how blessed we were. It was no longer Tim and I against the world, as the first surgery had felt. We now felt we had a small army beside us, ready do battle along with us.

I am sure that we still have quite a road before us, but after this week I know this: God still does miracles, I am blessed to know Joshua, life sometimes just needs some perspective, and friendships are an incredible blessing that teach us about God's unconditional love and comfort.

~ Through the Lens of Motherhood ~

Five days after Joshua was admitted into hospital, he was discharged. We packed his things quickly, almost afraid that the doctor would change her mind. We put Joshua into a wheelchair four times his size and stuffed pillows and blankets around him to keep him upright. Then we bundled him into the car seat. As we drove out of the parking garage into the sunshine, Joshua looked up and smiled.

We stayed at the hotel again that night and enjoyed a special evening with pizza, a movie, and sleeping in big beds. Although nothing could contain his joy, his scar was red and angry, he was shaking badly from withdrawal and weakness, and he still had a long road to recovery.

After dinner, Tim and I took Joshua to see Santa in the hotel lobby. Everyone who saw him sensed something special. Eyes followed Joshua—not eyes full of pity, but of anticipation. They could see his pain, his shaking, his weakness, and his painfully slow steps. They could see the large, red scar, but they also saw his clear, blue eyes full of joy and wonder. Santa had tears in his eyes, and he very gently held Joshua in his lap and chatted with him.

After visiting with Santa, we walked a for a little bit around the lobby. (Walking after surgery is vital, because it allows the lungs to clear of fluid and prevents complications like pneumonia.) Joshua stood in front of the Christmas tree, with his huge eyes watching the twinkling lights sparkle. As he stood there, the chef who had been watching him came out of the kitchen with a chef's hat for him, causing Josh's smile to grow even larger. Everyone smiled, and many had misty eyes. People seemed to know that there was something very special happening that night with this child in front of them. This little blue-eyed boy who had stolen my heart was truly a miracle, and I prayed that I would never doubt again the power of our maker and his ability to answer the prayers of his children.

After watching the tree for a while, I took Joshua back to our room, and Tim ordered a movie. Joshua sat on the bed and watched the movie for a while, and we gave him more of his pain medication. A little later there was a knock on the door, and one of the hotel staff had gifts from Santa and his elves—a blue dinosaur, milk and cookies, and a big bunch of balloons. That dinosaur still sits on Joshua's bed, a small reminder of the night God moved a hotel full of people with compassion for a little boy with shaky legs, a big red scar, and blue eyes full of joy and wonder.

We didn't end up sleeping in that hotel, as nice and fun as it would have been. Joshua was just too excited, and with his pain medication kicking in, he wanted to jump on the beds and run around. We decided that it was time to go home. That night he woke in the night needing medicine only once, and before he'd even swallowed it, he was back asleep.

I had gone into the week mentally prepared for the worst-case scenario; for the first time on this journey I'd lost my optimism. It was my signature on the consent form, so if anything happened to him, I would live with that knowledge for the rest of my life. As I sat there in the waiting room for all those hours, I began to fully understand that this wasn't a fixable or curable problem. It wasn't a disease that, once removed, would be healed. His heart was broken, and you can only repair, replace, patch, and hope that science comes up with a longer-lasting solution. It really is about buying him time, and it's about quality of life. My hope for more, my optimism, was useless, and I had to come to terms with it.

As I thought back to Joshua sitting on Santa's knee, obviously still in pain and his shaking hands holding on tight to the Christmas bells, his sunken eyes filled with delight, I knew that this child was the miracle all along. The steps we have to take to prolong his life are all part of that one miracle: Joshua. God's gift to me that Christmas was giving me my belief back, no longer blind belief wrapped in my desires for a perfect outcome, but a real and lasting belief in miracles, because no matter what we face with either of the boys, all I have to do is look at them to see the miracle.

The Saturday morning after discharge was nothing like the joy of the day before. Gone was the magical and delighted boy. Joshua woke up screaming in pain. At 3:00 a.m. I gave him his medicine, and he managed to get back to sleep. He woke up again at 7:30, wailing in agony. We brought him downstairs to the couch, but he wouldn't move, wouldn't drink, and wouldn't eat. We watched his favourite movies and tempted him with his favourite foods. He was no longer the happy boy trying to jump off the hotel bed. In his place was a sad and empty-eyed little boy whose silence filled the room.

If I pulled off his shirt, he'd hold his hands over the scar to hide the ugly marks, and with his eyes closed he'd yell "no" until I put his shirt back down. I tried to explain the scar, the pain, and that the worst was over, but he was so young, and he just didn't believe it. His sad eyes persisted. While the wait for the surgery had been hard, it was the days afterward that proved to be even worse. But things improved, slowly, but after a few days, Joshua was slowly walking around again, and he'd begun to eat. He needed less pain medication, and as the days went by, he started to grace us with that beautiful smile again. Life is a roller coaster; you just need to hang on, do your best not vomit when it gets too twisty, and enjoy the rush of the dips and plunges.

TWENTY

My parents brought Kaleb back to us on the Sunday after Joshua was released. He'd only been gone for one week, but when I had him back in my arms, it was like he'd been missing for weeks. I'd been so busy worrying about Joshua that I hadn't had time to really think about Kaleb, but his smiles and crawling and cruising were fun to watch and a much-needed distraction. Joshua wasn't interested, and it seemed as if he was suffering from post-surgery depression. Our experience throughout Joshua's second open-heart surgery was so different from the first.

The days leading up to Josh's second surgery were filled with an outpouring of love, prayers, meals, hospital visits, hotel gifts, and hundreds of emails, texts, and phone calls. It wasn't a nice time in our lives, but looking back, I can see how far God had brought me. The second surgery allowed us as a family to really see the church as a loving community that longs to hold us up when the storms come. They don't want us to hide in our own pain, afraid to show them who we really are. Rather, they want to help, to be told how to help, to see our pain and hurt, and to walk beside us. I was starting a very long journey of understanding that I didn't need to pretend or hide. It would take years to figure out, but the first moments of insight started during the time of the second surgery.

Tim preached a sermon once about prayer. He explained that "Abba" means "Daddy," and he gave us the image of a child who is close to his father. How do they communicate with each other? While neither of my kids were talking yet, there was no doubt they had a beautiful relationship with their father, both searching for him if he left the room. Without words, they were able to maintain a deep, loving, and fulfilling relationship with each other. It made me think that this is how our Abba wants us—seeking him out, running to him with arms wide open as he watches and loves us in spite of our mistakes.

In the months after the surgery, we slowly began to achieve a quiet, peaceful existence, but the disruptions came at night. One of the outcomes of Joshua's stroke was severe language impairment; even with therapy, he still wasn't saying more than a word here or there. He knew my name and other small words, but communicating was very hard. Not being able to communicate his fears and pain led him to have horrific nightmares. Every night. For months, his blood-curdling screams shook our house and woke us multiple times a night. It was only within that year that we managed to get him to talk to us with some feeling words, and "scared" was the one he picked most often.

The boys were growing. Kaleb was now running and keeping up with his brother at the park, and he was beginning to show his unique personality. We got memberships at the zoo and Science Centre, and we celebrated birthdays with parties and "happy cake." Joshua worked on his speech therapy and very slowly began to speak, one word at a time. Kaleb was renamed Kaper by his brother (a mashup of "brother" and "Kaleb"), and our fears for Josh's heart began to ease. His right side was weak, causing him to fall easily and experience difficulty with his fine motor skills and speech. Our developmental pediatrician met him once and believed that Joshua had autistic spectrum disorder. In spite of everything I told her about Josh, it seemed like she made his behaviour fit that diagnosis, and I soon realized she wasn't listening to his history.

By then Joshua was also beginning to learn the alphabet and count to ten and back again. Although he wasn't talking, his intelligence was clear, and he was engaging with us and making eye contact. Not spectrum behaviour at all. Returning to SickKids, I spoke with the stroke team and begged them to help. They put us on to a child psychologist who agreed that Joshua was not autistic, although he definitely had problems. They would need to test him but not until he was four. In the meantime, she promised to write a letter stating that he was not autistic and that his medical history could account for his many delays. Between the stroke and all the general anesthetics, not to mention the days of non-development time while sedated or on life-support, it seemed to make sense that he was behind.

Fighting for Joshua in this new way, with all the phone calls and hours spent in therapy and different doctors' offices, taught me something that both eased my soul and helped me use my voice more effectively—not to hurt or bubble over in pure frustration or anger, but to be helpful and healing. Sometimes it meant speaking up and saying how I felt, and I didn't always do that beautifully, but I was beginning to try. Holding things in hadn't been healthy for me, and it wasn't going to serve my children well in the years to come. It remains a learning process for me.

Kaleb had an incident requiring brief hospitalization, IV fluids, and breathing assistance. As a healthy, active two-year-old, he squirmed and tried to pull out his IV, and the nurse was clearly annoyed. When something happens that upsets me, I need to share it in order to process my feelings, but when I talked about this, I was told that I was complaining. The message I repeatedly received was that I needed to keep my thoughts and feelings to myself, to be "more Christian." I questioned again what that meant, and I also started hiding myself again, which led to social anxiety that, up until recently, I didn't even know I had.

As we moved through this new stage of finding balance in our life between church, the kids, my own work, and the full-time job of caring for two sick children, I started to become stronger, more confident, and more sure of my role as their mom. I wouldn't allow certain things to happen. I wasn't going to sit back and do nothing because I was afraid someone wouldn't like what I had to say. I was tired of stifling my emotions, and I'd learned the hard way that it wasn't a healthy reaction to life.

My anger was changing, so slowly at first that I didn't notice. It became less explosive and more internal. I told myself that I was better, stronger, or "over it." I developed a more open prayer life, and I began to talk more freely through my blog about my feelings. As I found healthier outlets for my anger, I felt a deep change. I could hear something hurtful and not blow up but rather accept the hurt feeling in the belief that I deserved it. It was a strange mental place, because it was buried so deep my subconscious, I truly believed I was doing better.

I often heard the word "grace" during this time—as in, it was something I didn't have. But during this period of learning how to advocate for my kids, I discovered that grace means being truthful in love, not hurting or humiliating people, or placing blame. Grace speaks with love and compassion. I had to speak up for my boys many times during those early years, but I learned to do so with love, and as a result, many of the therapists, doctors, and later teachers have become friends. The difficulty for me is my identity being rooted not in how God sees me, but in how others see me. My challenge is to be rooted in how God, not others, view me.

TWENTY-ONE

I'VE WRITTEN ABOUT JOSHUA'S HEALTH, MY OWN MENTAL HEALTH, AND the healing journey we've been on, but I haven't mentioned much about Kaleb, other than to say he has asthma and allergies. That's because he deserves a chapter of his own for the lessons he and God have taught me. Through him I found healing from some of the heartache surrounding Joshua's birth. Just being able to feed him allowed for that immediate bond. Kaleb is strong, funny, sweet, affectionate, smart, creative, and fun. He said "Mama" the same week that Joshua did, and he's the most enthusiastic greeter when we walk into the room.

He also has asthma. His breathing sometimes becomes so ragged that he looks desperate. With every cold or allergy episode comes the fear that an asthma attack will follow, and he's permanently shackled to an EpiPen and a puffer. Summer's humidity leaves deep circles under his eyes; his coughing is ceaseless, and his mood edgy. He refuses food during these times and has occasionally gone with very little food for a number of days. I've had to learn to be calm, clear-headed, and patient.

One day Kaleb woke up sick; I thought he had a cold, not knowing yet that he had asthma. He was feverish, so when he wanted to lie down all morning, I wasn't too concerned. A friend was coming over for coffee that day, but as the appointed time drew closer, I got more concerned about Kaleb. He was lethargic and his coughing was making him vomit, which was causing dehydration. Then he turned blue. I was gripped with the old fear that had choked me in the CCCU as Joshua lay blue and lifeless. My first thought was that maybe he had a misdiagnosed heart problem, so I made an emergency appointment to see the doctor. I asked my friend if she would come with me to stay with Joshua while I took Kaleb in.

When we arrived at the doctor's office, the doctor said that Kaleb was very sick and needed to get to the hospital. She called the ER and told them to expect us. My friend, Joshua, and I raced Kaleb across the street to the ER. I phoned Tim to let him know what was going on and then made my way through the maze of rooms to find Kaleb. When I entered the room, I saw him lying motionless on the bed, an oxygen mask pushing air into his lungs.

I grew up with asthma in my life. My sister and my mother had it. My mother had spent almost a year of her life at SickKids in an oxygen tent because of it. Asthma I was familiar with; I knew it could be managed with meds. But Kaleb is not a good patient. He hasn't suffered like Joshua, so he fights it, and being in the hospital with him was a nightmare.

We did everything we could to keep it under control, but some nights Kaleb would wake up unable to catch his breath. My mother's advice would come back to me: stay calm and don't let him see you panic. As I held him close, I told him he was okay, rubbed his back, showed him how to take deep breaths, and then held him until the panic eased. When the worst would be over and he would fall back to sleep, I would quietly leave his room. As I'd close the door, I'd notice my shaking hands.

People sometimes assume that you get used to it, that it gets easier, or that you get stronger. They're right, you get used to it. You learn tricks that make it a little easier, and you get stronger in many ways, but at the heart of it all you're still their mom, and they're still your babies. When they hurt, when they fear, when they cry or struggle, you don't leave the room unaffected. You just learn to keep calm on the outside and not show the panic. It's still there, though, and when all is said and done, you walk away with shaking hands and a racing heart.

Because of Joshua's speech problems there was silence in our home, and it wasn't until Kaleb began to speak that Joshua rose to the challenge. Kaleb, in his way, was helping Joshua to heal. Slowly we started to hear chatter fill our home, and it brought with it a noisy peace and lots of smiles and laughs.

TWENTY-TWO

Just before Kaleb's asthma attack, Joshua had another echo and a clinical check-up on the valves. The situation was dire. His heart was rejecting the new pulmonary valve, something that shouldn't have happened for ten to fifteen years. The tricuspid valve was no better. We were once again walked through the open-heart surgery conversation. By now, it was becoming my norm. You can't alter the path a congenital heart defect takes you on, no matter how hard you fight it. On the day we brought Kaleb home from hospital after his asthma attack, I got a phone call from the surgeon to say they had booked Joshua's surgery for just one week later. Just one week to explain it to him, one week to understand it ourselves. One week to plan, one week to "deny" that it was happening, one week to gather the emotional strength that was absolutely necessary.

But for that one day, we allowed ourselves to forget and enjoy time as a family. We headed to the airshow and the CNE and ended up at the roller coaster at Ontario Place. The kids were exhausted by the time we got home, but they still had enough energy to head out to the back yard for a game of "fly" with Daddy. Watching Joshua fly through the air, all smiles, brought a lump to the throat, knowing that in a few days we wouldn't be able to toss him around the way he loves. By the time the game was finished, Joshua was so tired he became lethargic, wouldn't eat, and finally wanted his bed at 6:00.

With the house quiet, Tim and I were left with the knowing. The next morning, I would head out the door with Joshua and make the trek to SickKids for our pre-op appointment. He would have blood tests, chest X-rays, and a duplex scan. Then we'd sit and talk with the surgeon, learn what to expect (by now I think we can skip that part), and then make the trip home with a little boy who knows what's coming. There would be no more hiding; he was going hear the surgeon and us.

He knew what the tests meant and he'd do his best to distract us to get our attention off the surgeon's words. He'd bring toys to us and act silly to make us smile, and he might even close his eyes and pretend he isn't there. Nothing he did, though, would stop what was about to happen. Nothing I did would be able to put a halt to the pain about to come. I would leave after again signing consent for them to cut into Joshua's chest and stop his heart. There is no running or hiding from that reality, I had learned that by then. As hard as it was to acknowledge, we knew it was necessary. His heart failure wouldn't get get better without help. All that was left was trying to find the right words, words he would know and recognize that would help comfort him.

I would tell him repeatedly that God could hear him without him needing words. God would know what he needed, and he would comfort him if he was scared. Joshua would only need to trust his friend. My hope and prayer was that he could understand what I was telling him, I so badly hoped that he understood enough to know peace and comfort from the knowledge that his friend and maker would be with him no matter what. I couldn't think of any other way to help him.

The first thing Tim and I did that morning was sit down on Joshua's bed and fill him in on what would happen that day, doing our best to assure him that we loved him, this was all going to make him feel better in the end, and he would hear some scary things but afterward he would come home with us. He seemed okay, though it was hard to know what he was thinking when he couldn't talk or share his feelings and fears. Tim drove us to the hospital and dropped us off, then he went home with Kaleb and waited for the babysitter before coming back to join us.

Joshua was booked for a number of tests. The first was a blood test, and as soon as they took his blood, he began to cry—not so much in pain but in knowledge. He closed his eyes as tightly as he could and sobbed. He continued to sob all the way to the chest X-ray area, where he put his head in my lap, holding tightly to my hand and his monkey. They called us in for the X-ray, and he sat where he was supposed to sit and did everything he was supposed to do without being asked. As we left, he once again began to sob. It wasn't until we got to the clinic and found some toys that I managed to distract him long enough to stop the sad crying.

We were next taken to a room where we met with a nurse who asked all the requisite questions, and then the resident surgeon came in to explain the surgery. Joshua tried everything he could think of to distract me from what the doctor was saying, until finally Tim arrived and I was able to play with Joshua while Tim listened to the doctor. The resident was the same one who'd sat in on his last surgery less than a year earlier, and he was able to go over in detail every aspect of his previous surgery, and then explain the new surgery, the risks, the fears, and the hopes. He couldn't answer our most pressing question, which was why this continued to happen to Joshua. No one, not even the one of the best surgeons in the world, could figure out why his pulmonary valve was no longer functioning. They all just said they were very surprised and hoped it didn't happen again. All the information, all the statistics were laid out, then they handed over a pen and asked us to sign on the dotted line.

The statistics are always scary for me. I hated math; numbers make little to no sense to me, but ever since Joshua's stroke, I pay close attention to the numbers. As before, the chances of Joshua dying on the table was one in twenty. We signed. What else were we supposed to do?

Joshua had a duplex scan and watched *Dora the Explorer*, and then we went back upstairs for a talk with our surgeon, one of the very best cardiothoracic surgeons in the world with a specialty in complex congenital heart defects. He again went over the statistics with us and shared his ideas on repair, complex surgery, or a full replacement. He explained that we would likely need the replacement but that he wanted to do everything he could to prevent that from happening. A complex surgery wasn't as likely, since they needed to take tissue from his heart sack and, since this was his third surgery, there likely wouldn't be any "good" tissue to use. (A complex surgery means that they create a valve from his own heart tissues.) It all sounded terrifying. Throughout all the tests, talks, and explanations, Joshua held my hand tightly, both of our fingers left white from the lack of blood flow, but his tears at least had stopped.

We took the train home, and Joshua sat beside me with his head resting on my shoulder, his blue eyes sad, his beautiful smile gone. Before bed I asked him if he wanted to talk about the day, but he didn't respond. I explained that in order to make him feel better, they needed to do an operation. It would hurt and be scary, but Mommy and Daddy and God would be with him the entire time. We'd take very good care of him, and when it was over, we'd bring him home with us. He listened with his eyes closed. Then I asked if he wanted to talk anymore or if Mommy should stop, and he simply said "stop." We watched an episode of *Curious George* to cheer him up, and then I tucked him into bed. We said our prayers and had good-night kisses.

On September 6, 2011, we woke early, packed Joshua into the car, and made our way to SickKids. We followed the normal routine, with the doctor signing Joshua's chest in thick, black ink. As I stared at those initials this time, I saw not the ugly mark of the ink on white skin but rather the significance of the gesture. The doctor was signing his heart, making sure that Joshua didn't get lost in the system. He was keeping him safe from mistakes in the charts. I thought about our lives, of Joshua's life and Kaleb's and ultimately my own, and I could see how our hearts are all signed by God's own Son—not with the black ink of a Sharpie, but in his blood. We know that he calls us his own so that we aren't lost in the system. He knows where we are, and he's in charge of us and has been from the moment the first drop of blood was spilled. I looked at the initials on my son's chest in the same way from that day on; I could now see the beauty of the gesture. I could see beyond the horror of what was to come to the hands that were there to keep him as safe as possible while it happened.

This surgery was another attempt to fix the tricuspid valve and another replacement of the pulmonary valve. It was scary, yet I felt at peace. Though my heart ached, there was something to the routine, now so familiar, that comforted me. I had seen the worst of open-heart surgery, and I knew what to expect. I knew the ups and downs that would come in the days and weeks that followed this massive invasion of the body. The doctors' words were less scary, because we'd heard them before and survived. The anger that governed my soul in years past was now filled with an acceptance that God was in control, whatever the outcome. Joshua wasn't alone in that OR that day. God was standing over his bed, guiding the hands of one of the best surgeons in the world.

Joshua, although still not using more than two words in a sentence, was in a better place than the year before and could better articulate his needs. The surgery lasted six hours, and afterward he was taken to the CCCU, where he was on a ventilator. Unlike previous experiences, though, he was quickly weaned off it. When he first woke up, he looked at me, and though his eyes were scared and sad, his first words brought smiles to our faces. He wanted to watch *Curious George*.

The next day he was taken up to the step-down unit on 4D. Joshua was only one-day post-op when he sat up for the first time, and he drank almost right away. On day two of post-op, though still shaky and in pain, he was making his way down the hall from his room to the playroom. Friends once again got us a hotel room, and Tim and I took turns getting sleep away from the hospital. Joshua didn't get angry this time, but he had a sadness that continued for two weeks. After only five days post-op, we were home again, Joshua on the couch watching movies, with the dog doing silent guard duty beside him.

The nightmares started up again, terrifying screams in the night that continued for months and got progressively worse as time went on. Just three weeks post-op, Joshua began his first day of pre-school. He loved his school, and he thrived there. Soon he was spelling his name, recognizing words, and getting a better idea of how to use words to communicate. He began talking regularly using two, and sometimes three, words strung together. In every way he seemed to have bounced back from that surgery with only the slightest blip on the radar. It was only at night that the reality of all he had been through tore through our peace and kept him from sleep. At night we all relived the horror that is called CHD and the trauma he'd been through. During the day he played with his brother, fought with his brother, and was the smiling, happy boy we'd always known him to be.

Joshua became associated with a few organizations at this time, including Cardiac Kids, Starlight Foundation, and the SickKids Foundation, for which he became an ambassador. They gave him tickets to the Toronto Maple Leafs' games. One night while driving to the game at the Air Canada Centre (ACC), Joshua finally found a voice to share with me some of the night terrors that plagued him.

On the way to the game, with insane traffic that stretched the ten-minute journey into an hour-long one, we talked about silly stuff, arguing and giggling about his age. Night was falling outside, and as it grew darker, Joshua said he was scared. After I probed a little, he told me: "Joshua scared dragon."

"Is there a dragon in the dark?" I asked.

"Yes," he said with a sigh.

I asked what colour the dragon was, and he said red. When I asked where the dragon was, he said "over."

"He's flying over your bed?"

He was relieved to be understood. "Yes, dragon flying bed."

I smiled at him in the rearview mirror. "You're in luck, Joshua, because I happen to know a dragon slayer! Before you were born, Daddy was one of the best dragon slayers *ever*, so when we get home, I'll get Daddy to get out his sword, and you point out where the dragon is. We'll get rid of him once and for all, okay?"

As we drove home after the game, Joshua again said he was scared. We talked about the dragon slayer some more, but more importantly, we talked about the *biggest, baddest* Dragon Slayer, and how all we had to do was call out to him and he would come to help us, like when I couldn't find the car after the game and told Joshua we needed to pray. Josh, who was in my arms, said, "Jesus, find car," and we headed directly to the car.

When we got home, we told Tim about the game. As he removed Joshua's shoes, I asked Tim if he could take down his dragon slayer sword just one more time. (Thankfully, Tim didn't ask too many questions. He seemed to understand and accepted it as a normal request that I'd explain later.) Up the stairs we went, in search of a red dragon. Once in his room, we asked Joshua where the dragon was, and he pointed to his bed. Tim waved his sword, stabbed it, and finally caught that dragon in a big green garbage bag. The bag moved around a lot, as the dragon found himself trapped, so it was difficult for Tim to get the bag back downstairs. Joshua and I followed hand-in-hand. When Tim got outside, he released the dragon, and we all watched him fly away! One pesky dragon flew away forever, gone from our lives (and, we hoped, from our sleep).

As we tucked Joshua into bed that night (with big grins), we asked where the dragon was. This time he pointed outside. I reminded him to ask God for help if he needed to, and that Mommy and Daddy wouldn't let any dragons come back into the house. I went to sleep that night more thankful than *any other* time in my life for that traffic jam that had given Joshua the time and opportunity to share something that had clearly been bothering him for some time.

Growing up, I often heard the story of my mom, sister, and grandma driving down the road when my sister, who was quite young at the time, started screaming hysterically to stop the car. My mom stopped immediately and turned to my sister to see what was wrong with her. My sister then asked, "Didn't you see the man?" When my mom probed, she learned that my sister had seen a man standing in the road. My mom and gran never saw the man, but they always believed it had been an angel standing in the road that day.

One day in particular I was feeling pretty low. I spent time in prayer during the afternoon, asking for comfort and hope, praying for something I couldn't even name. Bedtime came, and as I was tucking Joshua in and giving him his nighttime kiss, he sat up and pointed to the end of the bed and repeatedly said, "man." Chills ran up my spine, as this wasn't a word he'd used before. Could it be that God had sent an angel to watch over my son? Did Joshua see an angel that night? I don't know.

I tucked Joshua in tight and said, "If there's a man there, Joshua, then it's your angel that God has sent to keep watch over you tonight, someone who will keep you safe and offer you rest." After that, Joshua lay down and gave me a kiss. We didn't hear from him for the rest of the night—not one bad dream, no screams in the night. The house was silent.

TWENTY-THREE

With Joshua's heart issues set aside for the moment, we started filling his and Kaleb's days with fun. Moments of peace came upon us after dealing with the dragons; the frequency of the nightmares decreased, and sleep came into our home. We planned a family trip to Disney World. We made weekend trips to Niagara Falls, the zoo, parks, and museums. Life was returning to normal, speech therapy resumed, and Joshua was busy between school, therapy, and different ambassador jobs for the SickKids Foundation.

I told Joshua's story to a group of strangers in a downtown hotel while he sat quietly beside me eating a cookie. Telling the story brought all the emotions back, but I saw that the pain once etched into every fibre of my being was no longer that sharp stab but a dull ache. All that was left were the memories of pain, and when I lay down to sleep, I no longer wrestled with monsters. The friends who saw us through the last two surgeries became friends for life. Gone was the feeling of indebtedness; it had been replaced by a deep and abiding love.

While living in Europe, I worked in the kitchen of a castle that was part study centre and part conference centre. People came from all over Europe for either a ski holiday, a retreat, or to study theology. My job was to feed them. I lived in the small town in the valley, away from the castle in the mountains, and I had no car. It meant a long trek up the mountain every morning to be at work at six. Being a night owl, I usually struggled to get to work on time, and often I'd begin the climb up that "hill" with my eyes half closed.

One morning after a particularly late night, I walked the quiet streets toward the path up the mountain. Only the town baker and I were awake. About a third of the way to the castle I sat down on a bench to rest. In winter, the valley is often shrouded in fog so dense that from above it looks like a lake. That morning the sun was just rising, the valley was full of this thick fog, and all the colours of the rainbow reflected off it. It was so beautiful, the sunrise refracting all around. In that moment, I felt as though it was all for me, that God had wanted me to share this moment with him. Having kids has been like experiencing that sunrise breaking through the fog after a hard path taken.

One Sunday while Tim and I were on a trip to Vancouver, we went to St. John's Shaughnessy Church, and God spoke to me. Rather than sitting in the dark, as I assumed I'd been doing, I realized that I'd been hunkered down in the shadow of the cross. Walking through this valley of the shadow of evil, which is exactly what the journey with Josh's illness had been, I'd experienced new hope in the gifts God has in store for us. He doesn't promise a life without pain, but he promises to walk with us through it. I don't know how the story with Joshua's heart defect, Kaleb's asthma and allergies, or the suffering we've all been through will end. Learning that is a journey in itself, and it's the greatest blessing in my life. It brings me closer to God and opens my eyes to his gifts, miracles, beauty, majesty, sovereignty, and deep, unconditional love.

TWENTY-FOUR

THE TRANSFORMATION FROM CHUBBY, CUDDLY BABY TO LANKY LITTLE BOY running through the house and wreaking havoc can happen overnight. When this happened with Joshua, we rejoiced to see him progress, overjoyed that he was alive. When it happened with Kaleb, it was a somewhat painful change, and I lamented the loss of the baby years Watching my boys grow and looking ahead, I realize these children, all of our children, are merely on loan to us. Our job is to give them the wings and then let them fly.

All of our stories are fluid, journeys filled with moments of joy, grief, hope, and despair, moments of sharing with God and moments of silence with Him. Until I breathe my last breath, I will be moving along a road that has ups and downs, but my hope and prayer is that the sections that are moving away from God become smaller. The more I learn about God, the closer I come to realizing his character and discovering who he is. I will trust more, love more, and feel left behind less, doubt less, fear less.

Every once in a while, you see, hear, or remember something that changes your life. It either touches some deep emotional longing, ignites a passion you didn't know you had, or brings a part of you back to life that maybe you hadn't realized was dying. That happened to me when I finally submitted to baptism, when my husband signed me with the cross and called me Christ's own. I was indeed Christ's daughter, and I'd always believed it, but that day as I felt Tim's finger move over my forehead, I realized that my certainty in that knowledge had been on snooze for far too long.

Over those years in which I spent so much time in battle—fighting, hoping, dreaming, wishing, and praying for things to go my way—I'd forgotten that we're sometimes called to a different path than the one we'd planned. I was reminded again that divine love has brought me here with a destination in mind, because I am Christ's own, a beloved princess of the King, and I will not now or ever be forgotten or abandoned.

We can't promise our kids a "happily ever after," because we live in a broken world where anything can happen. I can, however, teach them how to grow strong in adversity rather than crumble under its weight, how to hang on to hope rather than give in to despair, how to reach out in prayer rather than turn away in anger, and how to use their gifts and love to help others who need it rather than selfishly hoard it for themselves. I can teach them about the one who saves, the one who promises that while this world can't offer peace, he can, and one day he will offer them the ultimate "happily ever after."

TWENTY-FIVE

WHAT IS NORMAL? A COLD, FLU, OR FATIGUE ALL SHARE SYMPTOMS WITH a failing heart. I once thought motherhood would be pretty easy, that it was mostly fun with a bit of work thrown in. I imagined playtime, parks, picnics, and then some trying teenage years mixed in with school and homework worries. I never bargained that motherhood would make me grow up. Whereas I was once irresponsible, I had to learn responsibility. Whereas once I hated routine, I had to embrace it. Whereas I used to thrive in my selfishness, I had to learn to be selfless.

No job, no photograph or photo shoot will ever satisfy me the way watching these two boys grow, learn, and become individuals does. Through the motherhood lens, I see more clearly who God has called me to be, a lesson that took time to learn and required work, pain, and experience. As the boys grow and we face new challenges and fears, he will always lead us back to the cross. He will always lead us home. Being a mom has taught me more about hope, prayer, the wonder of childhood, and God himself than any other experience I've gone through.

Tim had taken on a new ministry at a new church, so we said good-bye to our old and faithful church. In many ways, life continued as normal. We stayed in the same home, and the boys continued in their daily routines, but it was very different. Joshua was at new appointments every day for language therapy, occupational and physiotherapy, and repeated echos, Holter tests, blood work, and stroke assessments.

Three-year-old Kaleb went to his grandparents' house almost every day so that I could shuttle Joshua to doctors and therapists. In February 2013, we said goodbye to our old church and began a new ministry, one we were very excited about in a church across town. Leaving behind the safety of a community that had been so faithful to us was difficult.

Kaleb was visibly struggling with feelings of neglect. He was moody, difficult, and very clingy. He didn't understand what was happening in our home, and he couldn't understand the shift that happened when we began to see a decline in Joshua. He became tired and grumpy. We explained it away with excuses, thinking that he had cold, was tired, or maybe school was too much for him. Joshua's illness affected our whole family with its stormy clouds.

Joshua's therapy sessions were also taking a toll, and he began to dread them. Some days he cried all the way to a session, quiet sobs in the back seat, little whispers that there were just too many doctors. On one of those days when we were headed to the language therapist, I finally got into the back seat with him and did my best to explain his stroke. I told him all about his brain and how the brain works, and that sometimes if an injury occurs in the brain, it can take a long time to heal. I told him that all the doctors were working hard to fix him, that I was praying for him, and that his brain would heal. I reminded him that in September when he'd started school, he'd cried every night because he couldn't talk, but now he had friends at the school, and his talking was getting better. I talked to him about his physiotherapy that would help the weak side of his body gain strength so that one day he could run without falling. Yet still the tears spilled over, and though he remained silent, he wouldn't get out of the car until I promised to ask the therapist to shorten the appointment.

Therapy days were mostly the same. He was just too tired to face them. As we moved further into 2013, it became clear that a lot of things were becoming too much for him. In September, he had run the whole way to school. By January, I had to buy a wagon to pull him behind me. And by March, he'd come home from school and not be able to do anything more than sit on the couch for a few hours before once again trying to face the rest of the day. His decline was swift, and it finally forced our hand and made us call our doctor again. She brought him in immediately, and the results were once again not good. In past surgeries, they had attempted and failed to correct a secondary defect alongside his pulmonary defect. In fact, the repairs made in his last surgery made any more repairs impossible. Our options were fast running out. The doctor told us that more surgery was necessary, but she would discuss with the team to see what they could do.

In April of 2013, we learned that Joshua would need another surgery, but they didn't know how best to approach it. We'd already tried repairing the tricuspid valve, and Joshua's body continued to reject the pulmonary valves for unknown reasons. They decided to give Joshua another catheterization to get a better idea of what was going on in his heart.

The night we got the news we were headed to the Toronto Maple Leafs' game, and I remember not wanting to go. I just wanted to sit in my room, preferably in the dark, yell at God, and generally annoy him until I got answers. But when you have kids, you hold all this back until they're in bed. That night, Tim and I and my dad took Joshua to the game as planned, sitting in the box hosted by David Clarkson (who played for the NJ Devils at the time) and Cardiac Kids. And we pretended. We smiled, and eventually those smiles turned genuine in the light of Joshua's joy at being there. David Clarkson's mother invited us down to the ice, where Joshua was given a signed stick from David. He knelt down and chatted with Joshua for a while, and when we left the game that night, we felt a little better than when we'd arrived.

I often hear from people who have no idea what it's like to be surrounded day in and day out with therapy, medication, and impending surgeries that it must be nice to get all the perks from places like Cardiac

Kids and Starlight. They're right, but not for the reasons they think. It's the chance for Joshua to fully enjoy being a kid for one night—no doctors, no therapists, no pain, no negatives. Joshua had reached a point in April when playing at the park was nearly impossible, because within minutes he would be sweating and out of breath, too tired to continue. He would sit on the sidelines and watch while his friends raced up and down the slide. We'd go home every day with a heavy step, me trying to cheer him up with the platitudes I swear against, and him getting annoyed with me.

One day while we were walking home, a boy ran past. Joshua stopped to watch and commented on how fast the boy was running. I tried to move him along, but he forced me to stop. "I can't run fast," he whispered.

I got down on one knee and touched his shoulder. "It's okay, Joshua."

"Stop saying it's okay," he angrily responded. "It's not!"

I sat down on the sidewalk and looked at him. He was right; it's not okay, and it's not fair. Instead of sitting with him in that pain, I was trying to avoid the conversation. "I know, Josh. It's not okay. You get tired easily because you have a leaky heart. It makes you tired faster, and it's not fair."

Throughout the therapy sessions and medical appointments, Joshua continued to struggle with balance issues. He still walked on his tiptoes, and his feet pointed out rather than straight, so he had trouble with his legs and his gait. The gait, combined with the toe walking and the high tone left from the stroke, made his ankle muscles too tight, which caused balance problems that made him fall frequently. We met with his physiotherapist and were told that they wanted to put him in casts for three weeks in an attempt to loosen the muscles and save him from a painful surgery and long recovery.

The prospect of the casts caused Joshua so much anxiety, he became angry, sad, fed up. His struggle made me turn again to God and ask when the suffering would end? Psalm 40 would run through my mind as I went into his room every night. After he'd fallen asleep, I'd touch his head and beg God to heal him, only to be met with silence.

Joshua was diagnosed at this time with severe receptive and expressive language impairment. We had him in therapy, but since it was expensive, we couldn't stay in it for an extended period of time. We received help from the Bishop's Company (a discretionary fund for the Bishop of Toronto), but Joshua needed intense therapy.

I heard about a school run out of the Bloorview Children's Rehab Hospital and applied, but everyone told me the spaces were incredibly limited and that children came from all over Canada and even the States. Our chances of getting him in were almost impossible. I knew that the two-year program was everything I could hope for. With on-site therapists, therapy was integrated into the daily school routine, which meant that when he left school for the day he could come home and be a kid. It also meant that I could stop shipping Kaleb off to babysitting. I could spend the time with him that we both so badly needed. Securing therapy for Joshua was a long and stressful process; I tried every possible option, but kept running into walls. This school was my last hope, yet the chances were so slim, I almost didn't go to the interview.

During the week we were waiting for the catheterization and struggling with therapy and the weightiness of his heart problems, I received a letter accepting him into the Bloorview program, which would focus mainly on language but also offered occupational and physiotherapy throughout his senior kindergarten and grade one years. That letter sits in my memory box in the basement to this day, and every once in a while when I start to wonder if God is here, if he can hear me, if he cares, I go down and pull it out again. With each reading I go back to that moment, and I know again the truth. He is here, he cares, and he hears me.

On May 21, 2013, I took Joshua for a routine pre-op for the catheterization, and we talked about what to expect during the appointment as well as the procedure a few days later. Joshua seemed to understand. Other than suggesting that the doctors tape his heart to fix it, he didn't have a lot to say. When asked if he was scared, he said, "No, the doctors will fix it." I asked if he had any questions, and he asked if he could bring his ball to bounce in the doctor's office.

During the appointment, Joshua became very interested in the plastic model of a heart on the desk. He asked if that was what his heart looked like, and then asked me to explain where on the model his own heart was broken. When the nurse came in, we discussed what the next day would look like. Although Joshua was playing with his Thomas, every so often he looked at the model. Then he stood up, came over to us, and asked me, "Did you fall when I was in your tummy and my heart got broke?"

I had to explain again that no one caused this to happen, that it wasn't anyone's fault. I told him that I was born with broken knees and needed surgery to fix them. I told him that Kaleb was born with broken lungs and needed medication to fix them, and again I tried to explain that things like this sometimes just happen. By then, both the nurse and I were teary-eyed. How does one explain this kind of thing to a child when you can barely figure it out for yourself? The question that day from his little lips reached down deep into my heart where I had hidden my deepest fears. Is this my fault? Was that stupid, unfriendly womb to blame? My throat ached with unshed tears for the rest of the day, and I felt guilt and shame clinging to me like the stench of a dirty diaper on the baby in your arms on a hot day.

After leaving the doctor's office, we headed downstairs to get the chest X-ray and blood tests. Joshua started with the questions, like, "Is it fixed yet?" Every doctor, technician, and nurse became the person who was potentially going to fix his heart. I lost count of the times I had to explain that it wasn't fixed yet and that it wouldn't be fixed the next day. I didn't know how to get his head around the fact that his heart will never be fixed, that he will always have a broken heart, and that every surgery or procedure is really just buying him more time.

With all of Joshua's questions and fears about life and death and who caused this to happen to him, we began a new step into our faith—teaching our son about the same faith that we clung to on a daily basis, teaching him that God would protect him and never leave him alone, that God would help him and comfort him. It wasn't an easy time for Joshua. He still struggled with nightmares every night. For weeks he would wake up screaming, usually multiple times a night.

Joshua was beginning to question faith and God. One night after being sad all day, he began to articulate a belief that God must be sleeping, because no matter how loud he prayed, God couldn't hear him.

That night more than any other I discovered that being a mom is one of the hardest jobs in the world. What I say in moments like these mattered so much more than all the kisses on the knee or hugs on the couch. That night our prayers were loud. We screamed from Josh's bed, "WAKE UP, GOD!" and I prayed like never before that God would reveal himself to Josh. It also made me think of something that I might be able to do for Josh, something tangible.

Josh's favourite colour is red, which is also the colour for congenital heart awareness. The night before Joshua's catheterization, I wrote and asked all the people who were praying for Joshua to take pictures of themselves wearing red and send them to me. Joshua's language still wasn't good enough to understand the concept of all these people around the world praying for him, but if he could see a visual representation of those prayers via the photos, then maybe he would understand. The response was nothing short of incredible. The following day, throughout the drive to SickKids, the waiting, the catheterization procedure, and the recovery time, my phone kept buzzing. With every new email or text came a new face, a new red shirt, a new prayer offered up on my son's behalf. When I was allowed to go into the recovery room, I showed Joshua the pictures one by one and explained what they meant. I read him the messages, and he watched. In his eyes I saw the moment when he began to understand, and a smile lit up his face.

On May 30, after his catheterization, I spoke with a psychologist about Joshua, his nightmares, and his constant questions about death. She told me to start changing my words, from "fixing the broken heart" to a "special heart that needed some help" to have more energy, like Mommy and Daddy. She suggested looking at pictures of a heart, getting him to draw pictures of things that make him feel happy, sad, or scared so that he had an avenue through which to share his concerns with us.

I thought these were great suggestions, and that day I told Joshua I'd spoken to a doctor who said that his heart was special. Joshua then asked to see a picture of a heart, so we googled it and looked at "Mommy's heart." He asked to see the special part of his heart, and he wanted to know where it was, so I tapped him on the chest. We started to draw. Happy was a train, and scared was a scribble that he said was a song. This surprised me, so I asked him to sing the scary song. He began to sing "Jesus Loves Me," the same song I sang every night to him. He said, "We have to change the song!" I thought I was mishearing him, so I sang it to him to see what happened. He got upset and said, "Change the song." I sat looking at him for a little while, trying to figure why that song was so scary. Could it be that he doubted its truth? Did the words remind him that he wasn't loved?

When I was in grade one, I would walk down a bike path to get to the babysitter's for lunch, and every day on that path I'd meet a boy named Chris, who was in grade three and seemed huge to me. He'd stop me and force me stand by the fence. He never actually hurt me, but the threat was there and I was terrified of him. He told me that if I ever told anyone about it, his dad, a cop, would arrest my mom and dad, and I believed him. Every night after supper, my dad would put a record on, always classical music. When I'd hear that music start, a knot would form deep in my belly, and I knew that soon it would be bedtime and then back to school. I learned to hate that music; to this day, I can't fully relax if classical is playing.

Was I over-thinking Joshua's reaction to that song? To those words? Was he just feeling the dread that comes when he knows it's time for me to leave the room and leave him in the dark, where the nightmares inevitably come? I don't have the answers, and I may never know. It didn't matter, though. I sang a different song and held him for a while. We continued to pray for the nightmares to stop, and he continued to believe that God must be busy or sleeping.

The results of the catheterization tests confirmed what we already knew: the tricuspid valve was causing trouble, the leak had grown, and the combination of the two failing valves was causing Joshua's main issues. He was again in heart failure, and the proposed solutions were a tricuspid replacement or the replacement plus a shunt.

TWENTY-SIX

DURING ALL THE WORRY OVER JOSH'S HEART, I STRUGGLED WITH THE guilt that I was failing Kaleb, that I wasn't showing him equal love and attention. I worried that his childhood memories would be about how Joshua was loved more, or how his parents weren't there for him. The siblings of very sick children are always left a little out of the loop, and most people forget to ask about them and how they're doing.

The questions gnawed at me. How many hours had I missed of Kaleb's young life because of his brother's appointments and deep needs? I could see how he would try to gain our attention, how he struggled to find a place in a family swallowed up by CHD, stroke, tests, surgeries, and therapy. The stress affected him too, but he was also forgotten in the wake of our busyness and stress. It seemed that all words of praise and encouragement were given to Joshua. It didn't really come as much of a surprise when the behaviour issues started and he began expressing things through anger. I didn't know what to do, but I knew in my heart that my youngest needed me and that he doubted my love.

One hospital-free day when Joshua was sad and required my time and attention, we did experiments with leaky cups to show why fixing a leak is so important. We spoke at length about his heart, the hospital, and his fears that he would go to sleep and not wake up. I was exhausted emotionally, completely drained of all energy to cope. Tim came home and needed the car to run church errands, and I was so relieved when he offered to take Kaleb with him. I felt so much guilt that day for the relief, for the lack of energy to be what Kaleb needed me to be.

I shared my thoughts in a blog post, and a few days later, someone left a bag on our front steps with a card and a gift in it for Kaleb. When I close my eyes I can still see the delight and surprise on his face when he got that gift, because he was so used to seeing Joshua get presents. When I gave it to him, he went to pass it on to Josh. But when I told him it was for him, his eyes grew huge and he asked, "For me?" With excited hands he pulled out the gifts and carried them with him for days. I believe that God used that moment and the kindness and generosity of someone to show Kaleb that he wasn't forgotten or invisible. He was loved. He also used that gift on the step to remind me that he loves Kaleb too, and he is looking after him.

One of the amazing things I've learned in life is that we adapt and change, and even if we don't want to, we grow. I ignored God's call on my life at an early age, and at times I even wished I hadn't been raised in a Christian home, because then I could do what I want without all the guilt. But now, so many years and troubles later, I cannot imagine what life would be like without God and his Son. It's not always comfortable, but it has changed and strengthened me, especially through this journey.

One night in the late spring of 2013, Joshua asked if he was going to die. Knife to heart, of course, but I managed to assure him that we would work hard to make sure that didn't happen. Having a heart-to-heart talk with your young child about death is something parents should never have to do, but we did it, because I believe that honesty is best—as long as it's couched in terms of God's mercy and grace. I told him that death wasn't something we need to be afraid of; it's the beginning for us, because we believe in and have a relationship with God. When it's time to die, we will close our eyes one last time on earth and wake up in the arms of Jesus. As we talked, I could feel the tension leave his body.

On Monday, May 27, 2013, we spent the day waiting for the doctors to decide the fate of our son. We did our best to distract ourselves, but it wasn't easy. I cleaned, and then cleaned again. I took the boys to school and played at the park with them, and then we came home to play with Play-Doh. But no matter what we did, the phone in my hand was a reminder of what we were waiting for, and my mood, though I tried to keep it light, was rubbing off on the boys.

I got the call that evening. After discussing it at length, the doctors were conflicted. They didn't have an answer, and they didn't know how to proceed. We now had two new option. We could replace the tricuspid and pulmonary valve again and hope Joshua didn't reject them. His history, they said, was an indicator of the future, and they weren't sure that replacing the valves would give him the long-term quality of life they were looking for. They were worried that we'd be back there again in a year, having yet another open-heart surgery.

The second option was called the Fontan procedure, in which they'd bypass the right side of his heart completely, leaving him with half a functioning heart. It was a palliative procedure. If the Fontan failed, it would not be fixable, and he'd need a full heart transplant. But it could also offer him a better quality of life for a longer period of time. The procedure was still relatively new, and they didn't have any good statistics on how many kids actually lived a long and full life with a Fontan. The doctors didn't know which was the best option, so they decided that as Joshua's parents, we would need to make the final call. It was my dad who pointed out that what they had actually done was give the final say to God.

I think back to the day in the fetal echo lab counselling room, when my big concerns were whether I'd be able to breastfeed and keep the midwife. I'm so thankful that I didn't know what lay ahead, and I thank God daily that I'm not as all-knowing as I once wished I was. Some things can only be handled one step at a time—the stroke, and all the subsequent problems Joshua continues to face as a result, and of course his heart, all coming down to a choice between a last-go at fixing it and palliative treatment. Having "heart transplant" brought into the discussion was a sickening transition to a place I didn't want to go, a place I was nowhere near ready to face or give any headspace to.

Earlier in the day when the boys had been playing with Play-Doh, I'd overheard Joshua say to Kaleb, "This is my heart; it's broken." He held up a ball of Play-Doh to show his brother.

Kaleb, not to be outdone, also made a ball of dough and placed it to his chest, saying, "I have a heart too."

Joshua responded with, "You have a fixed heart; don't break it."

Later that night, still reeling from the news, I thought about that conversation between brothers. I'd come to life-altering crossroads before. Going to Austria changed the course of my life and my faith. Saying yes to Tim changed my life forever. That night, the ache was overwhelming; my soul had been rocked. Tomorrow I knew we would figure out a way to move forward, but that night I was gutted with indecision and fear. Tomorrow I knew l would find God's peace, I would sit with Tim, and we would make a call for Josh's future. *But* that night I allowed myself time wallow in the shadows and grieve over ending up in that place.

Neither Tim nor I slept that night. We lay side by side in our silence, thinking and praying, waiting for an answer to come. From the very beginning I had been praying for a miracle, for total healing. I couldn't pray and ask God for total healing and then allow the doctors to alter the make-up of his heart so drastically that it couldn't ever be put back again. I had asked our doctor what she would do if this was her child, and she said she would do what she could live with if the worst case scenario happened. That was how I finally came to my decision, and I believe it's how Tim came to his. I knew that I wouldn't be able to live with myself if we didn't do everything we could to fix his heart before moving into palliative treatment. It was that simple in the end. If we lost Joshua, I would need to lay him to rest knowing that I had done everything in my power and tried every option to make him well.

We decided the next morning to go with the Hail Mary pass, meaning that Tim and I felt that we couldn't agree to the Fontan procedure when there was still hope that the replacement of those two valves might give him more time. Maybe he wouldn't reject these ones; maybe he'd get years out of them. His history didn't have to be an indicator of his future. There was always a chance that we'd be here again the following year, but what if we weren't? We left the door open for a convincing argument for the Fontan, and we were awaiting the opinion of a specialist who wouldn't be back until the following Monday, but we told our cardiologist that unless he had a strong opinion that made a lot of sense to us, we would choose to go with the two new valves.

A pastor once said to me, "If you're trying to discern God's will, sometimes you need to try to open the door, and if the door doesn't open, you know to turn around and try the other door." The door was opened and the specialist gave us a green light for the double valve replacement surgery. With the decision made, we began the task of getting ready. The surgery date was set for the last day of July. With summer on the horizon, we decided to do our best to make it as fun as possible, given our limited options.

With the move to the new church we came into a new situation as far as housing was concerned. The church owns a rectory next door, which was larger and would better suit our housing needs. It would also make Tim more accessible to the boys during the day. We didn't want to give up the house we owned, but the idea of a larger home so much closer to Tim was a great opportunity. Kaleb would be starting school in the fall, and I didn't want to move after school had started and transition him mid-way through the year. It meant that we were moving, and the only timing that would work was to move just days after Joshua's surgery. I had a house to pack and tenants to find for our house. Somewhere in there we had to fit time in to be with the boys, who needed us desperately that summer.

As Joshua's heart failure worsened, his moods dipped to new lows. He had four or five meltdowns a day. He was angry, and he hit and kicked more. Kaleb often took the brunt of his abuse. Kaleb was too young to understand any of the things happening that summer, so we found ourselves needing to pay more attention to him and offering more comfort than ever. I often found myself struggling with two very needy little boys. Somehow I managed to pack the entire house by the end of June so that we could have a few weeks of "summer" at the cottage before heading to Sick Kids' for the surgery. The cottage was a welcome respite from a horrible spring, but never far from our thoughts was what loomed on the horizon.

Our surgery date was changed three times, and each time our entire extended family had to change all of their plans in order to make it work, since they were in charge of Kaleb while we were in the hospital. At the same time, I started to get phone calls from every department involved in Joshua's care, because they needed pre-op information.

The "holiday" at the cottage was interrupted with numerous trips to SickKids for appointments. Then my grandfather (who lived at the cottage) caught a cold, and we were forced back home to avoid the boys getting sick, which could put off surgery indefinitely. At that point we went into isolation for the pre-op phase of our summer. The house had been packed, so there wasn't much to do. We couldn't have play dates because we couldn't be around other kids and risk anyone getting sick. We spent our days in the back yard, and more often than not watched movies and hid from the intense heat. It wasn't an easy time, to say the least.

At the beginning of this journey, I was very angry and felt alone. My faith was bottoming out, and I struggled with what I assumed was silence from God. That summer, I sat in a new place of understanding and peace that I didn't think possible all those years ago. Not once during that summer did I feel alone. In the midst of the suffering we were completely surrounded by love and prayer. The outpouring from friends, family, and strangers was beautiful.

I still received daily photos of people wearing red. People mailed us items such as red photos and red stuffed toys. One school group sent a large bag of handprints (all the kids had traced their hands on red paper) with handwritten notes to let Joshua know they were praying for him. Another group painted four large canvases with their names and handprints, again with promises of prayers. The emails flooded my inbox every day. Many of the pictures came from total strangers who wore red for Joshua and promised to pray. Every day we received proof of God's promise to look after us. It was a display of love and kindness that should be forever marked in history.

That summer I didn't question God; instead, I trusted him. I leaned on him for comfort, and I found it. I won't say I didn't get scared, or that I wasn't worried, anxious, and sad, or that I didn't have moments of self-pity. I did. I had moments of despair, but they were short-lived. When they came, I turned to God and shared my thoughts with him in ways I didn't know how when this all began. I once said that I was being met by silence, but I've learned that silence happens when someone is listening.

After a number of scheduling changes, Joshua's surgery was finalized for August 1, 2013. In some ways, the summer seemed to take forever, but looking back, the surgery was upon us in no time at all.

Of all the things our family has learned on this journey, the greatest is trust—trusting God, to be specific. It's not the easiest thing to do; in fact, it's the hardest part of putting our faith in God. I believe, yet on many days I try to take control back, especially when my trust is slipping. But we're always brought back to that one question: Do you trust me? The answer is sometimes given with a gulp or a sigh.

Yesterday was pre-op. There are tests and questions to answer, and lots of waiting. Then the moment comes when you're face-to-face with the surgeon, and in the face of all your anxiety, you hear that whisper: "Do you trust me?" The moment when the surgeon runs through all the horrible things that could happen, all of your largest fears laid out for you on paper in black and white. That moment when you look and see words like "stroke," "vein perforation," "blood transfusion," "infection," "death." Then he hands you a pen and asks you to sign your name, giving them permission to take all these risks with your son. That's the moment when you come face to face with God and have to answer the hardest question of faith: Do you trust me?

There was a time during our journey when I couldn't bring myself to sign that form. I'd force Tim to do it, because those risks were just too much for me to give permission for. I had to look God in the face and answer, "No, I don't think I do trust you enough." Things have changed in my life; I have seen that growth happens slowly over time. I can look at all those horrible things and face those fears, because along the way I've come to know three things: God loves Joshua much more than I do. He loves me much more than I ever imagined, and he has a plan to redeem the pain we have all faced. I don't know what that will look like in the end; I can only say that I hope it turns out the way I want it to. But I know this—when God whispered "Do you trust me?" yesterday, I took the pen, signed the form, and whispered "yes" back.

~ Through the Lens of Motherhood~

On August 1, we once again put Joshua into the car. Kaleb was safely in bed at his grandparents' house. Usually the trip to the hospital on surgery day was a forlorn and devastating drive, but that day we were at peace. We got Joshua washed with his special pink soap and dressed in the hospital gown. We signed a new consent form, chatted with the surgeon, who shared his own misgivings about the choice we'd made, and again watched as the anesthesiologist signed Joshua's chest. When the time came, we went down to the now very familiar OR staging area and handed Joshua over to the care of the surgeons.

We got through the surgery feeling like we'd scaled a mountain and were now on the other side. When we'd handed Joshua to the OR team, I immediately had two lines of a song going through my head: "This is where the healing begins; this is where the healing starts," complete with the tune and everything. I didn't know the song, so I don't know where it came from, but it was significant. It didn't say that he is healed, but that this is where the healing *begins*; this is where the healing *starts*.

Overall the surgery went well. He had the two valves replaced and there were *no leaks*. He had never avoided leaks before. We felt so much peace and comfort, and we had more strength to handle the muckiness of the post-op period, which proved far less than ideal. Joshua experienced a collapsed lung; he was in pain and moaning in his sleep from it. His breathing was shallow, which made him "desat," meaning that his O2 saturation levels got too low when he was taken off O2. He couldn't keep anything down and spent the first few nights throwing up. His monitors and ventilator were thumping, and he just kept moaning. There's nothing worse than not being able to help your child through pain so bad he can't breathe, or that makes him hyperventilate and vomit. It's the most helpless feeling, yet somehow we found that when we needed it, we had the strength.

This was where the healing would begin, not end. We still had a road to travel. Every day he would get a little bit stronger. He'd keep fighting, because he's still a warrior with a warrior heart. He was still up to his old tricks and pulled out his own NG tube one morning, then he walked through his pain to take himself to the bathroom rather than pee in a diaper.

The Sunday after the surgery, Tim went to church while I stayed with Joshua. We were exhausted, and Joshua had gone through a really rough night. The sadness was returning, and we couldn't manage to get a smile out of him. I was struggling with plain "tired sadness."

When Tim returned from church, he gave me a card that had been given to him. He told me that when he walked out of the back room to the sanctuary, he was faced with a sea of red. The congregation had all worn red shirts as a sign of solidarity and prayer for our family. Tim had to choke back tears as he stood before our new community. This new church, which didn't really know us yet but had gathered together to show their support and love, meant the world to us. During the service a photo was taken and quickly sent to the local print shop, where they made a card and swiftly got it back before the service was over so that everyone could sign it and give it to Tim to bring to Joshua.

At that moment, the recovery became smoother. It was like the visual of the shirts— the knowledge of the prayers and support gave him the strength he needed to keep fighting and not get discouraged. He was allowed to go off the ward for short periods in a wheelchair, and we roamed the halls of the hospital, looking out at the summer sun through the windows. We shopped for a toy at the store downstairs, he enjoyed visits with some friends, Kaleb and his grandparents came, and by the end of the day, his smiles returned. Though he still had pain, his spirits were lifted, and I believe he got his hope back.

Kaleb, who for too long had struggled to understand what was happening, saw for himself how sick Joshua was. For the first time he seemed able to grasp that his brother's needs had to come first this time.

He walked into Joshua's room and saw him lying there with his large, red scar, still bloody and ugly looking. It was a shock to Kaleb, but as he stared, he very gently touched Joshua's hand and told him he missed him and hoped his ouchie got better soon.

I took Kaleb for a walk with me while Joshua visited with his grandparents. When it was time to leave, he didn't cry and cling as I'd feared he would. Instead, he kissed Joshua gently and then hugged and kissed me and told us both that he loved us. He then took Papa's hand and walked away. He matured that night; I saw it happen right in front of my eyes. With understanding came a deep compassion and love. That night we all slept as well as possible in a room filled with monitors, bells, and regular vitals checks by the nurses.

Once again, friends had lovingly arranged a hotel for us. Tim slept there at night and relieved me in the mornings so that I could catch a few hours before going back to the hospital. We were incredibly thankful for that hotel room. The Monday following that beautiful Sunday was just one day before we were to move into our new home. Tim spent most of the day at the old house making sure everything was packed and ready to go.

While Joshua and I sat in our room at SickKids doing his physio routine, our cardiologist came in for rounds. She smiled at me and said, "It's time to go home." I couldn't believe it. He was just four days post-op, and we were being released. Unfortunately, we had no home to return to, so Tim helped me get Joshua packed and wheeled down to the hotel, where we spent the night. The following day was moving day, and Joshua's bed was the first order of business. Joshua and I ordered breakfast in bed from room service. We walked the halls a little bit, and at three o'clock that afternoon, Tim called and said that he had the bed and couch set up for us and we could come to our new home.

This morning during worship time in church, I was reminded of how infinitely awesome our God is, how he can turn mourning to joy, and how he deserves all of our praise. He is life's oldest healer and greatest surgeon. The nights of sleeplessness are just now beginning to take their toll on Tim and me. The stress always hits us after it's over, and the same is true now just three weeks post-surgery. Our summer was spent gearing up for the worst set of circumstances, filled with stress, heartache, worries, and anxiety. I am happy to report that the last three weeks can only be described as an answer to prayer. The surgery was successful; we anticipate years before any more interventions will be needed. The nightmares that shook our home the first few nights have all but disappeared, and the pain is gone. Joshua's appetite has doubled; he's eating more than he's ever eaten before in his life. He's gaining energy and drive every day, and his emotional strength this time has been something of a surprise to me. He's much stronger than I knew, and I have always known how strong he is. Just last week I bought him a scooter, and yesterday he went around the block on it twice! (This may be normal for most five-year-olds, but for Joshua, who couldn't walk to the park just one month ago, this is a miracle!)

Kaleb took the entire separation in stride. He was cheerful, loving, and compassionate through the entire ordeal. If you ask him now, he'll tell you that you must be careful of Joshua's ouchie, and if Joshua allows him, he'll pull up Joshua's shirt to show it to you. It was the Kaper who worried me endlessly. I feared he would feel abandoned, left out, alone, hurt ... Instead, he proved me wrong and showed what an incredible kid we've been blessed with. He is by far one of the most compassionate little men I know.

This week we even made it to the cottage for a few days, and Joshua was able to swim again. At one point while sitting in the water and watching him and his brother playing, I couldn't help but think of how fast the last three weeks had gone. Joshua is a different kid in many ways. He's still recovering, he still tires easily, and there are days when he wants nothing more than to veg out. His scar is healing, but what once caused him shame he now proudly boasts about. His scar is now his symbol for "No leaks!" His smiles are brighter than they have been in a year.

Life has certainly changed in the Haughton house these past few weeks. God is indeed a good God. No matter what happens in this life, I have learned that there is nothing he can't do, and there *is indeed power in the prayers of his people. Congenital heart defects have no cure. Joshua still has a road ahead of him where his heart is concerned, and he still has years of language to get caught up on, but now more than ever I have the faith to believe in miracles. I believe that I can be strong and courageous when he is standing beside me, and even when it seems like it is impossible, with God, nothing is impossible."*

~ Through the Lens of Motherhood ~

When I look back to the beginning of our journey and remember the puss-infected wound that just wouldn't heal, and when I think of the hopeless silence and anger that took root in my heart, I can't believe God managed to get me to this place of healing and peace. When I see the journey from the other side, I see all the steps it took to get us here, and I know we couldn't have done it without a community of believers surrounding us in prayer, without family, without friends, or without each other. But more than any of that, I can't imagine doing it without the trust and hope we found in God. I can't fathom this journey without knowing that God was in control, without his guiding hand and comforting embrace. I couldn't imagine hope and healing without his gentle hand slowly working at cleaning the wound, knowing that one day I will discover that it's just a scar.

With the summer of 2013 at its close, the months of endless days turned into full days of school for both of the boys. It had been a long and at the same time very short summer. On August 28, Joshua had gone for his one-month post-op echo. The doctor had smiled and said that the regurgitation was so mild, it was almost not worth mentioning. The valves were not leaking. Just a month had passed since Joshua couldn't walk to the park without needing rest, and now he was racing around and keeping up with his brother. He was eating more than ever, and in September of that year, he began his next journey toward healing from the stroke at the Bloorview School. He excelled in that school and loved every second of it. He began talking in sentences, and by the end of his two-year program, they tested him again and told us that he no longer had a language impairment.

During his senior kindergarten year, he had a fall that required a call to 911, and we learned that he was having seizures in the stroke zone. He was diagnosed with epilepsy and began a new medication. He'd been having silent seizures for years without our knowledge; they kept him from a deep sleep and often prevented him from being able to fully concentrate. When he started the new medication, his language boomed, and soon it was no longer a matter of impairment but rather "catch up" mode.

When Joshua was seven, he had to have his tricuspid valve replaced again, but this time I convinced the doctors to try to do it in the catheterization lab. It was the first time that SickKids had done a valve replacement in that position on a child. Red shirts again began to pop up in emails and texts, and on the Sunday before the procedure, Joshua and I sat together in the pew of church and watched in awe as a sea of red shirts flooded the rows around us. As people made their way up to the communion rail, tears fell freely from my eyes. Joshua just sat with a huge smile on his face. The procedure went incredibly well, and after only three days in the hospital, Joshua was back at school and running around playing soccer at recess.

TWENTY-SEVEN

OUR STORY ISN'T OVER—NO ONE'S EVER REALLY IS. WE ALL STEP FORWARD and move into new phases of a journey; all of us are headed in one general direction, each moving forward and back as the stormy winds push at us. We learn, we grow, and sometimes we forget and need to learn again. This is my story; I need to have reminders all the time.

After a number of years, I was diagnosed with PTSD and found myself sitting in a dingy office and drinking lukewarm coffee while staring at a boring beige wall, trying to answer the question: What am I afraid of? I was forced to delve into dark places to discover the core fears that lay beneath the surface. In many ways, I was searching out that girl I'd buried long before—or that's what I thought when I started the process. But as I worked through the chaos, trying to find order and peace, I discovered that I hadn't actually liked that person very much; in fact, I hated her. What I needed more than anything else was to stop and consider what God says of me, and then choose to believe that. It's not about remaking myself, finding the old me again, or journeying to discover the new woman I see in the mirror each day. It's about asking

God to show me who I am and then accepting his answer as truth and living into that.

It takes time to heal and figure out the deeply-rooted feelings that have changed us over time. God asked me to be still and know that he is God, and recently I found out that the original Hebrew root of "be still" doesn't mean "be quiet" but "let go." He says to me, "Be still and know that I am God; let go and know that I am God." Let go of the fear, the worry, and the control, and allow me to work.

I've always believed that I had failed a test of sorts, because God had commanded me to be strong and courageous and have faith, but I hadn't. I had a deeply-rooted fear that I had somehow created this problem, that Joshua's suffering was somehow my fault. As I shared this with Tim, he told me to re-read the entire first chapter of Joshua, not just Joshua 1:9. I hate to admit this, but I was surprised. God tells Joshua that Moses has died; then he tells him to get up, because he has been chosen to lead Israel. He will be taking God's people into their new home. God lists off his promises for his people and all of the blessings he has in store for them. Then he says: "Just as I have been with Moses, I will be with you; I will not fail you or forsake you. Be strong and courageous, for you shall give this people possession of the land which I swore to their fathers to give to them" (Joshua 1:5-6).

First came the promises and the list of blessings, then came the reassurance that he could be strong and brave in light of those promises. It wasn't as I had created it in my mind: "Do this, then this, and act like this, and then I will do the impossible." I had it all backwards. God had been telling me "I will do this impossible thing," so relax, don't be anxious, be strong and courageous, because you can trust my promise. As I read through the chapter, I realized that God had done it, regardless of my weaknesses, my anxiety, my anger and my doubts, it was already done. So no, our story is not finished, and my faith journey continues to stretch me and change me, and it will until I breathe my last breath. The wounds are becoming scars, and scars tell of a battle fought and won. They emerge in an angry red, then turn white, and often jagged lines form across the wounded area. They shout out to those who see them: "Look what I have been through!" and "Look what I survived!"

I remember the first time Joshua went into surgery. Right before they took him in, I traced my finger down his still-perfect white chest, and I ached that it would never be perfect again. I mourned that loss long before we went into the OR that day. No longer would people look at Joshua and say, "He looks so perfect." Instead, they would see the line. My feelings when I look at the scar have changed over the years. Gone is the mourning, the sorrow, and the fear that someone will stare. Those feelings have been replaced with pride, because it screams: "I survived!" at me with every glance at his still-beautiful skin.

I hope to teach him to take pride in his battle scars; I hope that one day they will embody for him all that they do for me. I was in a plastic surgeon's office once for a routine biopsy. As I sat in the office, I noticed all the posters for creams that promised a miracle cure to make scars invisible. The doctor himself talked to me about what my scar would look like, and he promised to make it look good. It made me laugh; I remember after my first C-section being so upset about the scar. It bothered me horribly, but after my second C-section, I realized that it was proof of life. Proof that my boys came from my body, that I carried them, nurtured them, and gave them life. When I look at Joshua, I don't see an ugly red/white line. I see the symbols it represents, the bravery, the fight, the healing heart beneath.

When he looks at that scar now, the same one that has often caused him shame and embarrassment in the past, I hope that he sees what I see when I look at his marred yet beautiful chest and at my C-section scar. I see the proof of life.